THE LITTLE BOOK OF C#

HUW COLLINGBOURNE

bitwise books

The Little Book Of C#

ISBN: 978-1-913132-06-4

bitwise books is an imprint of **dark neon**

written by
Huw Collingbourne

DOWNLOAD THE SOURCE CODE

All the source code of the examples in this book may be downloaded (free) from the publisher's web site:
http://www.bitwisebooks.com/

Contents

Introduction

C# is the most popular language for .NET development on Windows. In this book I explain show you how to write C# programs and understand the main features of the language.

The C# (pronounced *'C-Sharp'*) language uses a syntax that derives ultimately from the C language. However, unlike C, the C# language is object oriented and it has many features, such as string data types and built-in memory management (garbage collection), which make many programing tasks simpler and less error-prone. In many respects it is closer to Java than to C.

However, whereas Java is primarily intended to be a cross-platform language whose programs can run just as well on Windows, Linux and macOS, C# was developed specifically for Windows development using the .NET framework. It is now also possible to develop and run C# on other platforms. However, this book concentrates on C# programming with .NET on Windows. The .NET 'framework' comprises a large library of programming code and tools to assist in creating and running programs. In this book I will explain both the syntax of the C# language itself and many of the core features of .NET.

Is C# Cross-platform?

In addition to being one of the most important and widely used languages for Windows development, C# can also be used to create web applications, mobile applications for iOS and Android and applications that run on macOS and Linux. C# is also used to program games using the popular Unity games engine. These cross-platform capabilities require the use of various additional tools and code libraries, however (see the Appendix) and won't be discussed in detail in this book.

Download the Source Code

All the source code shown in this book is available for download. The source code Zip archive contains code in the form of a single Visual Studio multi-project solution.

> **Download the code from the Bitwise Books web site at:**
> www.bitwisebooks.com

What Is In This Book?

This book begins with a gentle introduction to C#. Then it quickly moves on to more demanding topics: everything from C#'s object orientation to file-handling, exception-handling and generic collections. I know that there is plenty of information online about C# syntax and the .NET framework, and I haven't filled the pages of this book with all that readily-available information. Each of the books in *Little Book* series aims to give you *just the stuff you really need* to get straight to the heart of the matter without all the fluff and padding.

Who Should Read This Book?

This book is suitable for both beginners and more experienced programmers switching to C# from some other language such as C, Java, Ruby or Python. While C# can be used on different programming platforms, its real 'home' is Windows and its most complete development environment is Visual Studio. This book assumes, therefore, that you will program C# using Visual Studio on Windows. If you are a Windows programmer who needs a quick way to learn to program C#, this book is for you.

Making Sense of the Text

In **The Little Book Of C#**, any C# source code is written like this:

```
private void Greet(string aName) {
    textBox1.AppendText("Hello, " + aName + "!");
}
```

Some code may be preceded by a project name like this:

```
HelloWorld
private void Greet(string aName) {
    textBox1.AppendText("Hello, " + aName + "!");
}
```

This shows that the code can be found in the *HelloWorld* project in the folder of the source code archive related to the current chapter. To follow along with the tutorial, you can load the named project or solution into your copy of Visual Studio. See the section on *Using The Code Archive* in this Introduction for more information.

Any output that you may expect to see on screen when a program is run is shown like this:

```
Hello, Fred!
```

Explanatory notes (which generally provide some hints or give a more in-depth explanation of some point mentioned in the text) are shown like this:

This is a Note

This is an explanatory note. You can skip it if you like – but if you do so, you may miss something of interest…!

About the Author

Huw Collingbourne has been a programmer for more than 30 years. He is an online programming instructor with successful courses on C, C#, Java, Object Pascal, Ruby, JavaScript and other topics. For a full list of available courses be sure to visit the Bitwise Courses web site: http://bitwisecourses.com/

He is author of *The Little Book Of C*, *The Little Book Of Pointers* and *The Little Book Of Recursion* from Bitwise Books and *The Book Of Ruby* from No Starch Press. He is a well-known technology writer in the UK and has written numerous opinion and programming columns for a number of computer magazines, such as Computer Shopper, PC Pro, and PC Plus.

At various times Huw has been a magazine publisher, editor, and TV broadcaster. He has an MA in English from the University of Cambridge and holds a 2nd dan black belt in aikido, a martial art which he teaches in North Devon, UK.

About the Technical Editor

Dr. Dermot Hogan is a software developer who has led major projects written in Assembly Language, C , C# and a number of other programming languages. A specialist in real time trading technologies, he has managed and developed global risk management systems for several international banks and financial institutions. He is the lead developer of the independent software company, SapphireSteel Software. He holds a Ph.D in physics from the University of Cambridge. His current area of research is devoted to robotic control and imaging systems.

1 – Getting Started

This chapter explains what you need to do in order to get started with C# programming using Visual Studio and the source code archive that accompanies this book.

In order to develop and run C# programs you will need a set of tools including a C# compiler, the .NET framework and a C# programming editor or IDE (Integrated Development Environment). In this book I'll assume that you will be using Microsoft's Visual Studio environment on Windows.

Install Visual Studio

You may either use a commercial edition of Visual Studio or the free 'Community' edition. The Community edition has most of the same features as the commercial editions including the code editor, visual designer and integrated debugger. Visual Studio can be downloaded here: https://www.visualstudio.com/

Your First Program

In order to begin programming in Visual Studio, you need to select a programming language (C#) and a project type. Various different project types are available, as explained later in this chapter. Usually, in this book, we will be using the Windows Forms project types.

The New Project Dialog

You can choose a project type by making a selection from the *New Project* dialog. This dialog was changed in Visual Studio 2019. Here I will explain the steps needed to create a Windows Forms project, first using Visual Studio 2019, then using earlier versions of Visual Studio.

Visual Studio 2019

If you want to create a new project as soon as you start Visual Studio 2019…

- Start Visual Studio.
- In the Startup screen, select *Create A New Project*

If you don't want to create a new project at this stage, you can click 'Continue without code'. You can start a new project later on as explained below.

To start a new project from within Visual Studio…

- Select *File, New, Project*
- From the *Language* dropdown list, select *C#*
- From the *Platform* dropdown list, select *Windows*
- From the *Project Type* dropdown list, select *Desktop*
- From the project list select *Windows Forms App*

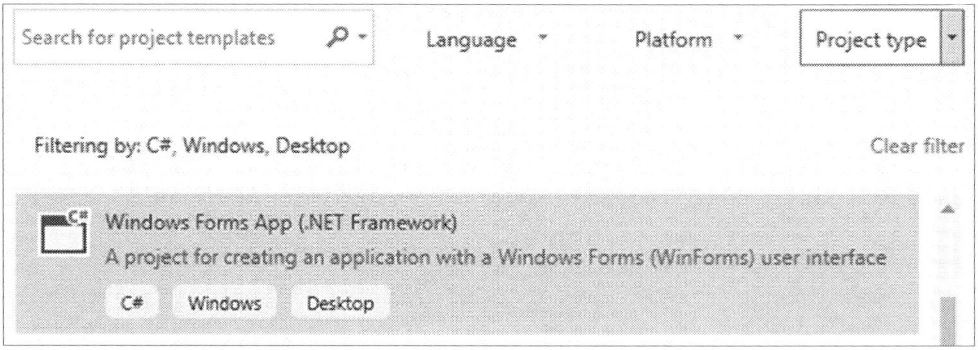

Alternatively, you can find the Windows Forms project type more quickly by using the search box on the *Create New Project* dialog and searching for **Winforms**.

- In the *Configure your new project* dialog enter the following details:
- In the *Project Name* field, enter a name for the project. I suggest: `HelloWorld`
- Next to the *Location* field Click the *Browse* button to find a location (a directory on disk) in which to save the project.
- Accept the default Solution Name (which should be the same as the project name) and Framework.
- Click *Create*

Other Versions of Visual Studio

If you are using a version of Visual Studio earlier than Visual Studio 2019, follow these steps start a new C# project.

- Start Visual Studio.
- Select *File*, *New*, *Project*

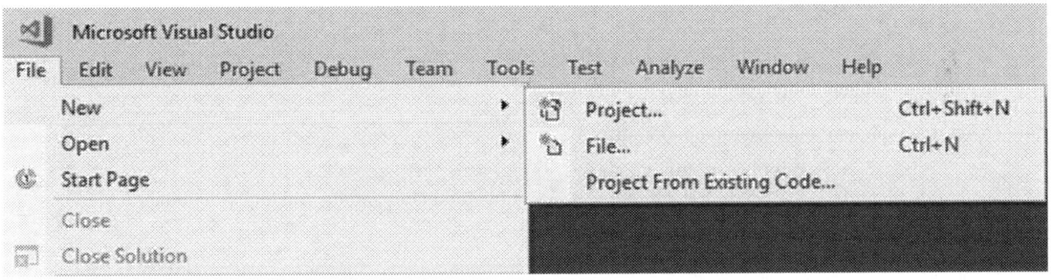

- In the left-hand pane, make sure Visual C# is selected.
- In the right-hand pane, select *Windows Forms App*

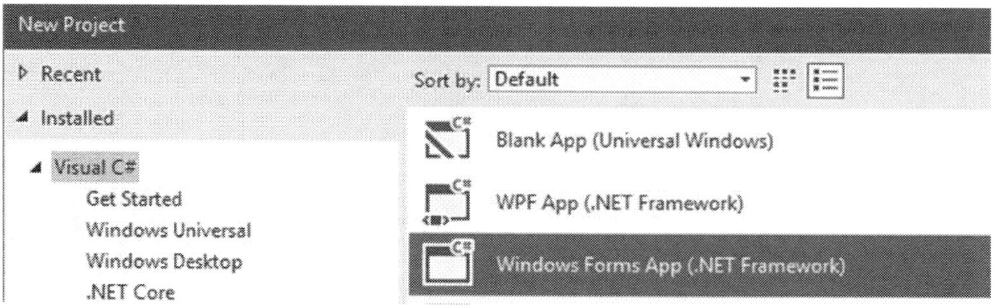

- In the *Name* field at the bottom of the dialog, enter a name for the project. I suggest: `HelloWorld`
- Click the *Browse* button to find a location (a directory on disk) in which to save the project.

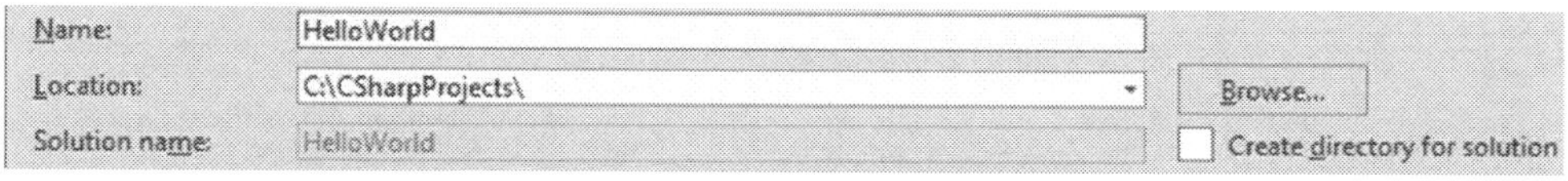

Selecting A Project Directory

You may want to store all your projects beneath a specific directory or 'folder'. Or you may click 'New Folder' at the top of the dialog to create a new directory. For example, you might create a directory on your C: drive called *\CSharpProjects*. Once you have located a directory, click the 'Select Folder' button.

- In the *New Project* dialog, verify that the *Name* and *Location* are correct then click OK.

All Versions of Visual Studio

Once you've created a new Windows Forms project, Visual Studio will show the project files in the in the Solution Explorer panel.

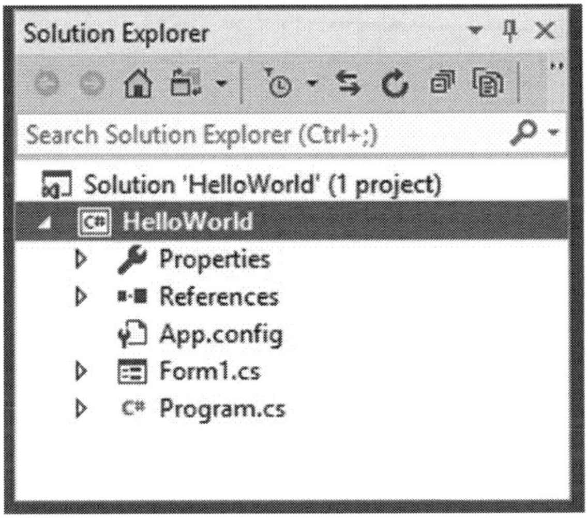

Projects and Solutions

Each Visual Studio project is included in a 'solution'. A solution may optionally contain more than one project.

You will now see a blank form in the centre of Visual Studio. This is where you will design the user interface. Make sure the Toolbox (containing ready-to-use 'controls' such as Button and Checkbox) is visible. Normally the Toolbox is shown at the left of the screen. If you can't see it, click the *View* menu then *Toolbox*.

- In the Toolbox, make sure the *Common Controls* section is expanded (click the 'arrow head' icon to the left of the label if necessary). Now click *Button*. Hold down the left mouse button to drag it onto the blank form. Release the mouse button to drop a button onto the form. The form should now contain a button labelled '*button1*'.
- In a similar way, drag and drop a *TextBox* from the Toolbox onto the form.

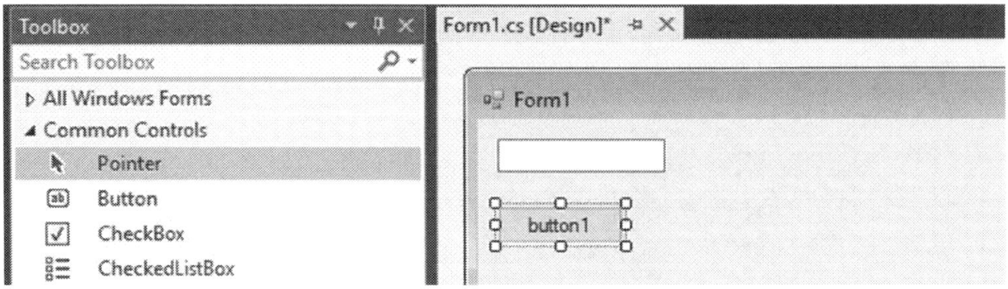

- On the form, double-click the *button1* Button. This will automatically create this block of C# code:

```
private void button1_Click(object sender,EventArgs e)
{

}
```

Don't worry what this all means for the time being. Just make sure your cursor is placed between the two curly brackets and type in this code:

```
textBox1.Text = "Hello world";
```

Make sure you type the code exactly as shown. In particular, make sure that the case of the letters is correct.

Case-sensitivity

C# is a 'case-sensitive' language. That means that it considers an uppercase letter such as 'T' to be different from a lowercase letter such as 't'. So if you entered `TextBox1.Text` you won't be able to run the program because the name of the `TextBox` control is `textBox1` which begins with a lowercase 't', so C# will fail to find a control called `TextBox1` with an uppercase 'T'.

The code shown above tells C# to display the words `"Hello world"` as the text inside `textBox1`. The complete code of this code block should now look like this:

HelloWorld

```
private void button1_Click(object sender,EventArgs e)
{
    textBox1.Text = "Hello world";
}
```

This code block is called a 'function' or 'method' and its name is `button1_click`. It will be run when the `button1` control is clicked. Let's try it out …

- Press CTRL+F5 to run the application (you can also run it by selecting the *Debug* menu then, *'Start Without Debugging'*).
- The form you designed will pop up in its own window.
- Click *button1*.
- "Hello World" should now appear as the text inside *textBox1*.
- Click the *close-button* (the 'X' at the right of the caption bar) to close the program and return to Visual Studio.

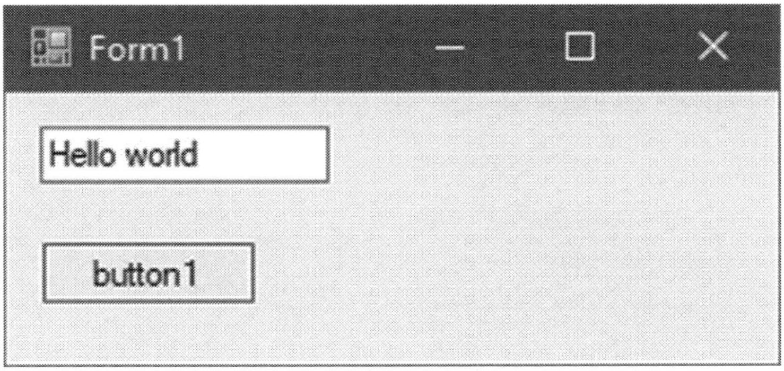

Source Code Formatting

In the code shown in the previous example, the opening curly bracket was placed on a new line following the name of the function:

```
private void button1_Click(object sender,EventArgs e)
{
    textBox1.Text = "Hello world";
}
```

In this book I generally prefer to place opening brackets on the same line as the function name (it makes better use of screen space) like this:

```
private void button1_Click(object sender,EventArgs e){
    textBox1.Text = "Hello world";
}
```

The code works in the same way whichever formatting option you prefer. Visual Studio makes it easy to change code formatting defaults by setting numerous options (select the *Tools* menu, then *Options*. In the *Options* dialog, go to *Text Editor*, then *Formatting*).

Visual Studio Overview

Visual Studio is Microsoft's 'integrated development environment' (IDE) for programming using C# and other programming languages. This screen shot identifies some important elements of Visual Studio.

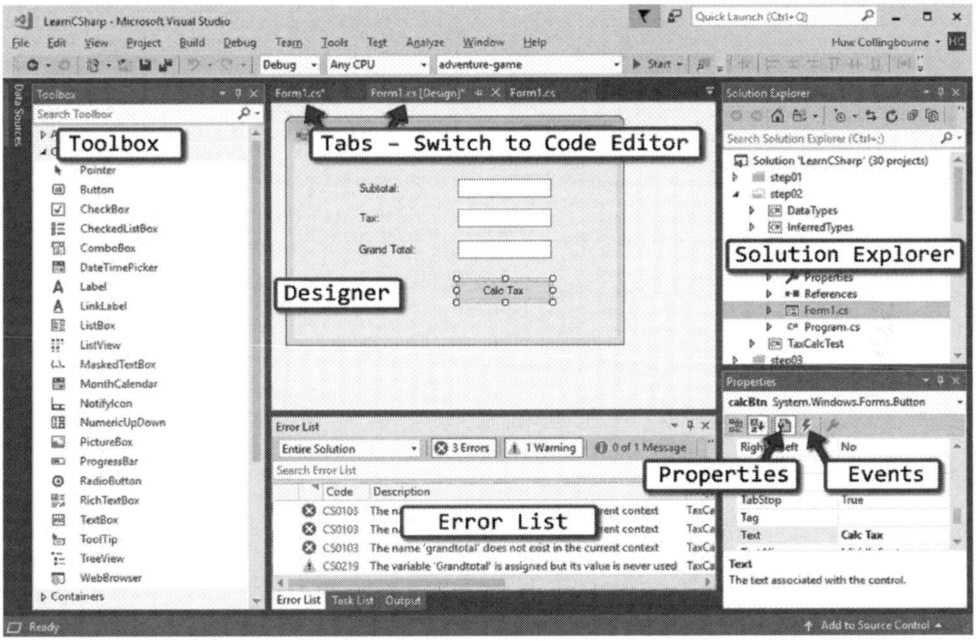

Toolbox	This contains components that can be dragged onto the form (user interface) which you are designing.
Tabs	Use the tabs to select a code file or the form designer which is indicated with the label '[*Design*]'
Designer	This is where you design a user interface. Select a component and pick an event from the *Events* panel to start coding.
Solution Explorer	A solution may contain more than one project. Right-click a project node and select '*Set as StartUp Project*' to activate it.
Error List	*Errors* (serious), *warnings* (less serious) and other messages relating to the code in your project are shown here.
Properties	Click the *Properties* icon to display and edit visual properties of the selected component.
Events	Click the *Events* icon to create and edit the code of 'event-handling' functions for the selected component.

Project Types

In Visual Studio, you are able to create a variety of different types of project using C#. These include:

Universal Windows Platform (UWP)

This provides support for creating applications across Windows 10 devices including PCs, tablets and phones.

Windows Presentation Foundation (WPF)

This provides support for configurable visual applications with styled components.

Windows Forms Application

This is used to create 'traditional' Windows applications with common controls such as buttons and text boxes.

Console Application

This is a 'non-visual' application that is intended to be run from the system prompt.

Why Do We Use Windows Forms?

In addition to the project types described above, Visual Studio also provides options to create more specialized sorts of project such as 'class libraries' and components. In this book, however, we shall usually be creating Windows Forms (WinForms) applications.

Windows Forms applications are much easier to create (by dragging and dropping components onto a 'form') than either WPF or UWP applications. Moreover, Windows Forms applications are supported by all versions of Visual Studio and Windows. UWP applications require Windows 10.

Don't be concerned about all the alternative project types that are available. The C# language – its syntax and behavior – works in the same way no matter what sort of application you are developing. This book aims to explain the C# *language*. You can apply the knowledge you learn to other types of C# development later on if you need to do so.

Solutions Containing Multiple Projects

As I mentioned earlier, a Visual Studio solution may contain more than one project. You can think of a solution as being a convenient way to group together related projects so that you don't have to keep loading projects one by one each time you need them. The file that contains a solution ends with the extension '*.sln*'. The file that contains a project ends with the extension '*.csproj*'.

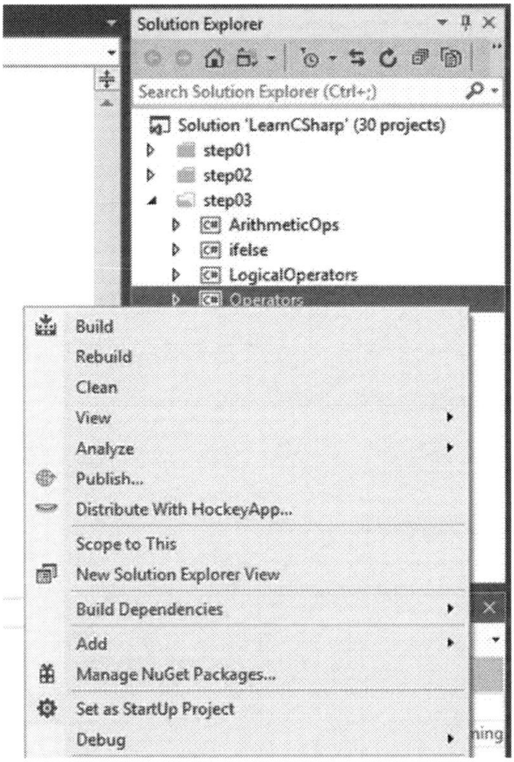

When a solution contains multiple projects, these are shown as 'nodes' in the Solution Explorer. Projects may also be grouped beneath 'folders'. Before compiling or running a specific project you need to set it as the startup project. You can do that by right-clicking the project node and selecting 'Set as StartUp Project' from the menu. Here I have loaded the *LearnCSharp* solution. I have selected the *Operators* project in the *step03* folder and I am setting it as the startup project.

Using The Code Archive

You may either load the projects from the code archive one by one (by selecting either the solution or project files from the subdirectories containing each project) or, as I recommend, you may load a solution that groups together all the sample projects.

This solution is called *LearnCSharp.sln* and it is found in the 'top-level' directory – that is the directory containing the subdirectories for each chapter in the book (*\Step02*, *\Step03* and so on). Remember that if you load the *LearnCSharp* solution you must be sure to set a startup project, as explained previously, before compiling and running a project.

Solution Folders

The *LearnCSharp* solution contains 'folders' of projects relating to each step of this course. The folders are shown as icons labeled *step01*, *step02* and so on. These 'solution folders' do not necessarily have the same structure as the folders (directories) on your disk. However, in the *LearnCSharp* solution I have arranged the solution folders to match the disk folders. When you are working on a specific step of the course just double-click a solution folder to show the projects it contains.

Compiling Projects

Before you can run a C# program you need to compile it. The C# compiler is a tool that translates the code you write into 'intermediate code' to provide instructions that can be executed by the C# 'runtime' system. The intermediate code is called CIL (Common Intermediate Language).

When your program runs, this CIL code is executed by a 'runtime environment' called the CLR (Common Language Runtime). That is why you must always 'build' or 'compile' your programs before they are run. Compiling is very easy in Visual Studio. Once a project has been set as the Startup project, you can simply select *Start without Debugging* from the *Debug* menu. This compiles and runs the current project. If there are any errors you will be notified and you will need to fix them before re-compiling. You can also compile all projects in a solution by selecting *Build Solution* from the *Build* menu.

2 – Features of the C# Language

> Every program is made up of some common elements such as keywords, functions and variables In this chapter, we look at the building blocks of C# programs.

When your programs do calculations or display some text, they use data. The data items each have a data *type*. For example, to do calculations you may use integer numbers such as 10 (of the `int` type) or floating point numbers such as 10.5 (of the `double` type).

Types

In C#, `int` is a 'type name' for integers. There are some other integer types too, capable of storing different ranges of values, but `int` is fine for our purposes. There are also several types that could be used to store floating point numbers such as `float` or `double`. In my programs, I will normally use `double` which is able to store much bigger ('double-precision', 64-bit) values than `float` (which is a 'single-precision', 32-bit value).

In a C# program you can assign values to named variables. Each variable must be declared with the appropriate data type. This is how to declare an integer variable called `myint` with the `int` data type and a floating point variable named `mydouble` with the `double` data-type (be sure to put the semicolon ; at the end of the declaration):

```
int myint;
double mydouble;
```

I can now assign integer and floating point values to these variables:

```
myint = 100;
mydouble = 100.75;
```

I must make sure that I only assign the correct type of data to each variable. This would be an error (my program would not compile):

```
myint = 100.75;
```

Alternatively, a value can be assigned at the same time that the variable is declared:

```
int myint = 100;
double mydouble = 100.75;
```

While there are many data types in C#, you will need to know these four from the outset. We will be using them frequently in the sample programs in this book:

`int`	an integer ('whole' number) such as 10
`double`	a floating point number such as 10.5
`char`	a character between single quotes such as `'a'`
`string`	one or more characters between double quotes such as `"a"` or `"abc123"`

You can see some example of variable declarations and assignments in the *DataTypes* sample project, which is included in the source code archive. This also shows how to use constants such as `TAXRATE` and how to calculate values such as `100.75 * TAXRATE` and assign the result to a variable. If you are new to programming, don't expect to understand this right away. Everything will be explained soon:

DataTypes

```
private void button1_Click(object sender, EventArgs e) {
    // These are constant values that can't be changed
    const string WARNING_MSG = "Warning! Do not change! ";
    const double TAXRATE = 0.2;
    // These are variables - they can be changed
    string mystring = "Hello world";
    char mychar = '!';
    int myint = 100;
    int someotherint;
    double mydouble = 100.75 * TAXRATE;
    string msg = "Goodbye";
    msg = WARNING_MSG + mystring + mychar + "\r\n";
    myint = 200;
    someotherint = myint * 2;
    textBox1.Text = msg;
    textBox1.AppendText("You owe: " + mydouble + " groats!");
}
```

Newlines

Newline characters are non–printing characters that insert a 'line-break' into text. In some cases, it may be sufficient to use a single newline character `'\n'`. With some controls such as a multiline text box, you need to use a pair of characters – a carriage return `'\r'` followed by a newline `'\n'`. NET also defines `Environment.NewLine` which is a special identifier that can be used to insert newlines and which will ensure compatibility across different operating systems. So, for example, I could have written this:

```
msg = WARNING_MSG + mystring + mychar + Environment.NewLine;
```

As we are not interested in cross-platform programming in this book, I will often insert these two characters when I want a newline in a string: `"\r\n"`. Chapter 6 has more to say on strings and special characters.

Variables

The value of a variable can be changed. So, for example, let's suppose you want to write a tax calculator that allows the user to enter a subtotal and then calculates both the tax and also the grand total (that is, the subtotal plus the tax). This event-handler function does that:

TaxCalcTest

```
private void calcBtn_Click(object sender, EventArgs e) {
    double subtotal = 0.0;
    double tax = 0.0;
    double grandtotal = 0.0;
    subtotal = 12.5;
    tax = 2.5;
    grandtotal = 15.0;
    subtotalTB.Text = subtotal.ToString();
    taxTB.Text = tax.ToString();
    grandTotalTB.Text = grandtotal.ToString();
}
```

Event-Handler Functions

Here `calcBtn_Click` is the name of the 'event-handling' function that contains the code that will run when a button named `calcBtn` is clicked. You can create an 'empty' event-handler function by selecting the `calcBtn` button on the form displayed in the Visual Studio designer. Then either double-click that button to create an event-handler for its default event (which happens to be the `Click` event), or select and double-click the `Click` event by name in the *Events* panel (see Chapter 1). Once the empty `calcBtn_Click` event-handler function has been created, you can add the code that you want to run when the button is clicked – which is what I've done here.

Here I declare three `double` variables named `subtotal`, `tax` and `grandtotal`.

```
double subtotal = 0.0;
double tax = 0.0;
double grandtotal = 0.0;
```

I have initially assigned the value 0.0 to each variable. But the whole point of a variable is that its value may *vary* – that is, once it has been given *one* value, it may be given a *different* value later on. My code assigns new values like this:

```
subtotal = 12.5;
tax = 2.5;
grandtotal = 15.0;
```

This simple tax calculator is limited to displaying the same values each time it's run which is, of course, not very useful. At the end of this chapter, we'll see how to create a tax calculator that calculates tax based on values entered by the user.

Constants

Sometimes you may want to make sure that a value *cannot* be changed. For example, if the tax rate is 20% you might declare a variable like this:

```
double TAXRATE = 0.2;
```

But now someone might accidentally set a different tax rate (this is not a problem in a very small program – but this sort of error can easily crop up in a real-world program that may contains tens or hundreds of thousands of lines of C# code). For example, it would be permissible to assign a new value of 30% like this:

```
TAXRATE = 0.3;
```

If you want to make sure that this cannot be done, you need to make `TAXRATE` a constant rather than a variable. A constant is an identifier whose value can only be assigned once. In C#, I can create a constant by placing the `const` keyword before the declaration as I have done in the *TaxCalc* project:

```
const double TAXRATE = 0.2;
```

If I try to assign a new value to this constant, I won't be able to compile my program. An error message will be shown and I will need to fix my code either by deleting the reassignment or by changing `TAXRATE` from a constant (by deleting the `const` keyword) to a variable.

Comments

Code can be documented using comments – lines of text which are ignored by the compiler. Multi-line comments may be placed between `/*` and `*/` delimiters, like this:

```
/*
    This function calculates
    tax at a rate of 20%
*/
```

In addition to multi-line comments, you may also add 'line comments' that begin with two slash characters `//` and extend to the end of the current line. Line comments may either comment out a full line or the 'trailing' part of a line which includes code before the `//` characters. This is an examples of a full-line comment:

```
// calculate and tax and grand total based on a subtotal
```

This is comment is placed after some code:

```
const double TAXRATE = 0.2;     // Tax rate at 20%
```

To comment out code that includes line comments, use the multi-line comment delimiters, /* and */:

```
/*
// calculate and display tax and grandtotal based on subtotal
const double TAXRATE = 0.2;     // a single-line comment
*/
```

To uncomment a multi-line comment block delimited by `/*` and `*/` you can put single-line comment characters `//` before each of the block-comment delimiters:

```
// /*
// calculate and display tax and grandtotal based on subtotal
const double TAXRATE = 0.2;     // this code is now un-commented!
// */
```

Keywords

C# defines a number of keywords that mean specific things to the language. You cannot use these keywords as the names of variables, constants or functions. Keywords include words such as `if`, `else`, `for`, `while` and the names of data types such as `char`, `double`, `int` and `string`. You can find a list of C# keywords the Appendix.

Statements

In C#, single statements are usually terminated with a semicolon `;` character. A statement is a small piece of code such as an assignment or a function-call. Here, for example, are four statements, each terminated with a semicolon:

```
textBox1.Clear();
sayHello();
greet("Mary");
someName = "Fred";
```

When you need several statements to execute one after another – for example, when some test evaluates to `true` (here I test if the `num` variable has a value of `100`), you may enclose the statements between a pair of curly brackets, like this:

```
if(num == 100) {
    textBox1.Clear();
    sayHello();
    greet("Mary");
    someName = "Fred";
}
```

Boolean values

In C# true and false (or 'Boolean') values are represented by the `bool` data type. When you perform a test in C#, it returns a `bool` which may either have the value `true` or `false`. Typically you won't explicitly initialize `bool` variables when performing tests, but you could if you wished to. For example, I could create a `bool` variable, `tf`, and assign it the value returned by the test `(x > 1)` which tests if the variable `x` has a value greater than 1:

```
bool tf;
int x = 10;
tf = (x > 1);
textBox1.Text = tf.ToString();
```

The final line of code here returns the string representation of the `tf` variable and shows this in a text box. Since `x` is greater than 1, this is what is displayed:

```
True
```

Functions

Typically you will divide your code into small named blocks or 'functions'. The names of functions must be followed by a pair of parentheses like this:

```
private void sayHello()
```

The start and end of a function is indicated with a pair of curly brackets and the code of the function is placed between those brackets, like this:

```
private void sayHello() {
    textBox1.AppendText("Hello\r\n");
}
```

If you want to be able to pass some kind of data to a function, you can add one or more 'parameters' between the parentheses. A function may return a value to the code that called the function after the keyword `return`. If (like the `sayHello()` function) it doesn't return a value the function name should be preceded with the keyword `void`. Here I have a function called `addNumbers()` which declares two `int` (integer) parameters called `num1` and `num2`. It returns a string that includes the sum of `num1` plus `num2`:

```
private string addNumbers(int num1, int num2) {
    return "The total is " + (num1 + num2);
}
```

private

The one thing I haven't explained yet is the `private` keyword placed before the functions shown in this chapter. The `private` keyword is called an 'access modifier' and it affects the 'visibility' of the function – that is, which other bits of code can 'see' and therefore get access to that function. For now, just accept that most of our functions will be `private`. I will explain functions, (or 'methods', to use the object-oriented terminology), in more detail in Chapter 4. Access modifiers are explained in Chapter 5.

namespace and using

At the top of a code file such as *Form1.cs* in the *DataTypes* project you will see these lines beginning with the keyword `using`:

DataTypes

```
using System;
using System.Windows.Forms;
```

The `using` directive gives the code in *Form1.cs* access to classes and types inside another code module or 'namespace'. When you create an application, Visual Studio adds the `using` statements you will need, at least initially.

Classes

Classes are the building blocks of object oriented programming. A class is like a blueprint for an object. For example, we could have a `Dog` class which defines all the features and behaviour of a dog. From that `Dog` class we could create individual dog objects called Fido, Bonzo and Cujo each of which shares the features (fur, tail, paws, etc.) and behaviour (eating and woofing) defined by the `Dog` class. We'll look at classes in detail in Chapter 5 which is all about Object Orientation.

This provides access to the `System` namespace:

```
using System;
```

When a namespace is used in this way, any classes inside it are accessible to the code in the current document. Look at this example:

Namespaces

```
using System;
using System.Windows.Forms;
using System.IO;


namespace Namespaces {
   public partial class Form1 : Form {
      public Form1() {
          InitializeComponent();
      }

   private void button1_Click(object sender, EventArgs e){
      int x;
      string currdir;
      x = 10;
      textBox1.Text = System.String.Format("x = {0}\r\n", x);
      currdir = Directory.GetCurrentDirectory();
      textBox1.AppendText("This is the current directory:" + currdir);
      }
   }
}
```

The System namespace contains a String class that has a Format() function. Since my code uses the System namespace, I can use String.Format() like this:

```
textBox1.Text = String.Format("x = {0}", x);
```

If you regularly need to use classes in a namespace, you should add that namespace to the using section. If you don't add the namespace, you may still be able to use a class it contains. But you will need to add the namespace (here, System) and a dot before the class name (here, String) in your code, like this:

```
System.String.Format("x = {0}\r\n", x);
```

In most of the simple programs described in the first few chapters of the book, the using statements will be automatically added for you by Visual Studio.

Scope

A namespace precisely defines the '*scope*' or 'visibility' of the code it contains. Some namespaces are nested inside other namespaces. For example, the IO namespace, which provides lots of useful code for dealing with disk files and directories, is nested inside the System namespace. One of the classes in the IO namespace is called Directory.

The Directory class provides various useful functions including one called GetCurrentDirectory(). Assuming I am using the System namespace, this is how I could use that function:

```
System.IO.Directory.GetCurrentDirectory();
```

If I need to use classes from the IO namespace frequently, I can simplify my code by adding this nested namespace to the using section like this:

```
using System.IO;
```

When I do that, I can use the Directory class without needing to qualify it by placing the System.IO in front of it, like this:

```
Directory.GetCurrentDirectory();
```

Type Conversion

Many classes and structures (*structs*) in the .NET framework include built-in conversion routines. For example, number structures such as the floating-point `Double` and the integer `Int16` include a function called `Parse()` which can convert a string into a number.

Structs

A `struct` is a data structure that encloses one or more 'fields' containing data items. For example, a struct might contain an employee record with fields to store each employee's first name, last name and salary. In some programming languages, structs are called 'records'.

Parse

In this example, I convert the string `"15.8"` to the `double` `15.8` and assign the result to the variable, `d`:

```
double d = Double.Parse("15.8");
```

This next example converts the string `"15"` to the `Int16` (16 bit integer) value, `15`, and assigns the result to the variable, `i`:

```
Int16 i = Int16.Parse("15");
```

But beware. If the string cannot be converted, an error occurs! This will cause an error:

```
Int16 i = Int16.Parse("hello");
```

ToString

Numeric types can be converted to Strings using the `ToString()` function placed after the variable name followed by a dot. Assuming that the `double` variable, `grandtotal`, has the value `16.5`, the following code will convert it to a string, `"16.5"`, and that string will be displayed as the `Text` item of the `TextBox` named `grandtotalTB`:

```
grandTotalTB.Text = grandtotal.ToString();
```

Note that .NET also has a class called `Convert` which can be used to convert between a broad range of different data types. For example, this converts, the `Text` (a string) in the `subtotalTB TextBox` to a `double`:

```
double subtotal = Convert.ToDouble(subtotalTB.Text);
```

This next example converts the value of the `subtotal` variable (a `double`) to a string and displays it in the `TextBox`, `subtotalTB`:

```
subtotalTB.Text = Convert.ToString(subtotal);
```

Alternative Conversion Routines

The *TaxCalc* sample project contains examples of various ways of converting between data types. You may want to edit the code in that project to try out alternative conversion routines.

Type Casting

I've decided that I want my tax calculator to display an integer version of the grand total in the title bar of the window. In order to 'round' a double value (dropping the floating point part) to an integer, I can 'cast' the double to an integer.

Cast

A cast is an instruction to the compiler to let you treat one data type as another type. The types must be compatible (for example, you can cast a floating point number to an integer number but you cannot cast a number to a string).

To cast one data type to another, you need to precede the variable name with the name of the target data type between parentheses. Here is how I would cast the `double` variable, `grandtotal` to an integer (`int`) and assign the resulting value to the `int` variable, `roundedtotal`:

```
roundedTotal = (int)grandtotal;
```

In general, converting data using a casts is less 'safe' than converting data using a function that has been specifically designed to do the conversion. That is because a function can try to deal with potential problems and return information if an error occurs. In the present case, therefore, instead of casting `grandtotal` to `int` I will once again use a function of the `Convert` class:

```
roundedTotal = Convert.ToInt32(grandtotal);
```

I convert this back to a string in order to display it in the title bar of the current program:

```
this.Text = roundedTotal.ToString();
```

this

The `this` keyword refers to the current object. Here the current object is the form (that is, the main window) of my tax calculator program, so `this.Text` sets the text shown in the title bar of the window.

Sample Program: Tax Calculator

Here is a complete version of the function that computes and displays the values when the button is clicked:

TaxCalc

```
private void calcBtn_Click(object sender, EventArgs e) {
      const double TAXRATE = 0.2;
      double subtotal = Double.Parse(subtotalTB.Text);
      double tax = subtotal * TAXRATE;
      double grandtotal = subtotal + tax;
      int roundedTotal;
      subtotalTB.Text = subtotal.ToString();
      taxTB.Text = tax.ToString();
      grandTotalTB.Text = grandtotal.ToString();
      roundedTotal = (int)grandtotal;
      this.Text = roundedTotal.ToString();
}
```

Notice that I have assigned values to the variables as I declare them. In some cases, the assigned value is the result of executing some code to do a calculation like this:

```
double tax = subtotal * TAXRATE;
```

Declaring and initializing variables all in one go like this has the benefit of making your code concise and also ensures that you never have any variables with unknown or unpredictable values. As an alternative, I could declare the variables first, like this:

```
double tax;
double grandtotal;
```

Then, later on, I can calculate and assign their values like this:

```
tax = subtotal * TAXRATE;
grandtotal = subtotal + tax;
```

In long and complex programs, it may be clearer if variables are declared all in one place, at the start of a function, and values are then assigned later on in that function.

Programming Style

Different programmers have differing views on what is 'good' or 'bad' programming style. There are no hard and fast rules. However, you should generally try to be clear and consistent. At the very least, I would strongly encourage you to declare all variables in one place, prior to using them. C# allows you to declare variables in the middle of executable code as I declare the variable `grandtotal` here:

```
subtotal = Double.Parse(subtotalTB.Text);
tax = subtotal * TAXRATE;
double grandtotal = subtotal + tax;
taxTB.Text = tax.ToString();
```

This can be confusing, however, especially in long code blocks. It is generally much clearer to declare all variables *before* the executable code of a function.

Uninitialized Variables

Using uninitialized variables in C# is not allowed. This code, for example, won't compile (because the `tax` variable is not initialized with a value):

```
double tax;
double grandtotal = 0.0;
subtotal = Double.Parse(subtotalTB.Text);
grandtotal = subtotal + tax;    // ERROR: tax not initialized
```

Later on, I assign *calculated* values to the variables:

```
subtotal = Double.Parse(subtotalTB.Text);
tax = subtotal * TAXRATE;
grandtotal = subtotal + tax;
roundedTotal = Convert.ToInt32(grandtotal);
```

Implicitly Typed Variables

C# lets you declare and initialize local variables without specifying a type. You must do this using the `var` keyword instead of a defined type, such as `int` or `double`, like this:

```
InferredTypes

var num = 100;
var num2 = 200.5;
var str = "Hello world";
```

C# infers the actual type from the data that is assigned to each variable. So if you assign a string, the variable will be given the `string` datatype. If you assign a double value it will be given the `double` data type and so on. If you are used to a language such as Ruby or Python where it is normal for variables to infer a datatype, this may seem like an attractive option in C#.

Be aware, though, that unlike Ruby or Python, once some data has been assigned to a variable, C# does not allow the *type* of a variable to be changed. For instance, if a `var` (implicitly typed) variable has been assigned a string value, that variable's data type becomes fixed as a string and it cannot subsequently be assigned any other type. This is *not* permitted:

```
var str = "Hello world";
str = 2;
```

Type inference in C# has no real benefit for many programming tasks. Type inference may, however, be useful for certain specialist types of data querying or looping operations which may be capable of returning more than one type.

Here is a very simple example of a `foreach` loop that iterates over an array (a sequential list - I will have much more to say about arrays in Chapter 6) containing a `string`, an `int` and a `double`. The loop defines the `thing` variable using the `var` keyword. At each turn through the loop, the `thing` variable infers the type of an array element:

```
foreach (var thing in somethings) {
   textBox1.AppendText(thing + " is a: " + thing.GetType() + "\r\n");
 }
```

This is the complete code that runs when `button1` is clicked in the *InferredTypes* project:

InferredTypes

```
private void button1_Click(object sender, EventArgs e) {
    var num = 100;
    var num2 = 200.5;
    var str = "Hello world";
    object[] somethings = { str, num, num2 };
    // str = 2; // Not allowed!
    textBox1.Text = str + " is a: " + str.GetType() + "\r\n";
    textBox1.AppendText(num + " is a: " + num.GetType() + "\r\n");
    textBox1.AppendText(num2 + " is a: " + num2.GetType() + "\r\n");
    textBox1.AppendText("--Loop through the array--\n");
    foreach (var thing in somethings) {
        textBox1.AppendText(thing + " is a: " + thing.GetType() + "\r\n");
    }
}
```

This is the output:

```
Hello world is a: System.String
100 is a: System.Int32
200.5 is a: System.Double
--Loop through the array--
Hello world is a: System.String
100 is a: System.Int32
200.5 is a: System.Double
```

3 – Tests and Operators

In this chapter we look at ways of running different bits of code depending on the results of tests. And we also look at operators – special symbols that are used to perform a number of different operations in C#.

Most computer programs have to make decisions to take different actions according to whether some condition is or is not true. C# can perform tests using the `if` statement.

if

An `if` statement is used to evaluate a test. The test itself is placed between parentheses and it should be capable of evaluating to `true` or `false`. If `true`, the statement, or block of statements, following the test is run. A single-expression statement is terminated by a semicolon. A multi-line block of statements must be enclosed within curly brackets.

IfElse

```
double someMoney;
someMoney = Double.Parse(textBox1.Text);
if (someMoney > 100.0) {
    MessageBox.Show("You have lots of money!");
}
```

The line of code enclosed between a pair of curly brackets is what I want to run:

```
{
    (MessageBox.Show("You have lots of money!");
}
```

But I only want the code to run, and display the string `"You have lots of money!"` if the value of the `someMoney` variable is greater than 100.0. This piece of code does this test:

```
someMoney > 100.0
```

Only if the test evaluates to `true` (that is if the value of `someMoney` *is* greater than 100.0) is the code within curly brackets run so that the message is displayed.

Test operators

You may use other operators to perform other tests. Here I use the 'greater than' operator (>) in a test:

```
if (someMoney > 100.0)
```

If I wanted to test if the variable was less than 100.0 I would use the 'less than' operator (<). The test would then be written as:

```
if (someMoney < 100.0)
```

I'll take a closer look at operators later in this chapter.

else

Optionally, an `else` section may follow the `if` section and this will run if the test evaluates to `false`. In this example, if the value of `someMoney` is greater than 100.0 the message `"You have lots of money!"` is shown. If it is 100.0 or less, the message, `"You need more money..."` is shown:

IfElse

```
if (someMoney > 100.00) {
    MessageBox.Show("You have lots of money!");
} else {
    MessageBox.Show("You need more money...");
}
```

When only one statement needs to be run after a test, you may optionally omit the enclosing curly brackets. So the code above could be rewritten like this:

```
if (someMoney > 100.00)
    MessageBox.Show("You have lots of money!");
else
    MessageBox.Show("You need more money...");
```

But be careful. If you omit the curly brackets around a set of statements, only the first statement is associated with the test condition.

For example, let’s assume you want to test if `x` is greater than 10. If the test succeeds you want to display the message `"Great news!"`, then assign 100 to `x` and display the message `"You’ve won $100"`. If the test fails, you want to do nothing. The code shown below works as expected because when `x` is 10 or less all the statements between curly brackets are skipped:

Ifelse

```
if (x > 10) {
    MessageBox.Show("Great news!");
    x = 100;
    MessageBox.Show("You've won $" + x);
}
```

But this code does *not* work as expected:

```
if (x > 10)
    MessageBox.Show("Great news!");
    x = 100;
    MessageBox.Show("You've won $" + x);
```

That’s because only *one* statement – the first line of code that follows the test – is skipped if the test fails. The other two lines are *not* associated with the test and they will, therefore, run both if the test succeeds and if it fails. That means that in all cases `x` is set to 100 and the message `"You’ve won $100"` is shown.

Unbracketed Code

If you don’t place curly brackets around the code you want to execute after a test, only the first line of code following the test will be executed. For reasons of clarity and consistency, I generally prefer to use curly brackets to enclose blocks of code to be executed following a test even if those blocks only contain a single statement. Here, for example, it is absolutely clear that only one line of code is associated with the test condition `(x > 10)`:

```
if (x > 10){
    MessageBox.Show("Great news!");
}
x = 100;
MessageBox.Show("You've won $" + x);
```

if…else if

You may also 'chain together' multiple `if…else if` sections so that when one test fails the next condition following `else if` will be tested. Here is an example:

Tests

```
if (userinput.Text == "") {
    output.Text = "You didn't enter anything";
} else if ((userinput.Text == "hello") || (userinput.Text == "hi")) {
    output.Text = "Hello to you too!";
} else {
    output.Text = "I don't understand that!";
}
```

Parentheses or no Parentheses?

Experienced programmers may object that I sometimes use parentheses where they are not needed. For example, look at this test :

```
if ((userinput.Text == "hello") || (userinput.Text == "hi"))
```

The parentheses are not syntactically required around the conditions `(userinput.Text == "hello")` and `(userinput.Text == "hi)` and the test would work just the same if they were removed, like this:

```
if (userinput.Text == "hello" || userinput.Text == "hi")
```

As we shall see, however, with more complex tests, when multiple test conditions are 'chained together', it is quite easy to make a mistake in the logic of a test. You can avoid many mistakes by always putting each 'sub test' such as `(userinput.Text == "hello")` inside parentheses. This isn't always necessary but it does no harm and it can save you from making silly mistakes accidentally.

The code shown above tests if the text box named `userinput` is empty (that is, if it contains an empty string `""`). If that test succeeds the message `"You didn't enter anything"` is displayed.

If, however, it fails because there *is* some text in the text box, the next test after `else if` is made. This uses the 'or' operator `||` to test if the text in `userinput` is either `"hello"` *or* `"hi"`. If this test succeeds, `"Hello to you too!"` is displayed. But if that test too fails then the code following the final `else` is run and, in this case, the string `"I don't understand that!"` is displayed.

switch

If you need to perform many tests, it is often quicker to write them as 'switch statements' instead of multiple `if...else if` tests. Here's an example:

Tests

```
switch(userinput.Text) {
     case "":
         output.Text = "You didn't enter anything";
         break;
     case "hello":
     case "hi":
         output.Text = "Hello to you too!";
         break;
     default:
         output.Text = "I don't understand that!";
         break;
}
```

In C# a switch statement begins with the keyword `switch` followed by a 'match expression' between parentheses. The match expression is some value to be tested. It can be any non-null value such as a string, a character or a number. Here I want to use the `Text` (a string) of the `userinput` text box:

```
switch (userinput.Text)
```

I can now test this against values in a number of 'switch sections' or 'case statements'. Each switch section begins with the `case` keyword then a value of the same data type as the match expression. Here the match expression is a string and my switch sections specify various strings – such as an empty string, or a specific string such as "hello".

The value in each switch section is compared with the match expression and, if a match is made, the code following the `case` keyword, the test value (such as the string `"hi")` and a colon is run:

```
case "hi":
    output.Text = "Hello to you too!";
```

When you want to exit the `switch` block you need to use the keyword `break`. If a `case` test is not followed by `break`, the code of all subsequent `case` tests will be executed one after the other until `break` is encountered. You may specify a `default` which will execute if no match is made by any of the `case` tests.

The entire switch block, including all of its switch (the `case` and `default`) statements is enclosed by a pair of curly brackets, with the opening bracket immediately following the match expression:

```
switch(userinput.Text) {
   // case and default sections go here
}
```

In the example code in the *Tests* project, if `userinput.Text` is an empty string (`""`), it matches the first `case` test and `"You didn't enter anything"` will be displayed. Then the keyword `break` is encountered so no more tests are done:

```
case "":
    output.Text = "You didn't enter anything";
    break;
```

If `userinput.Text` is either `"hello"` or `"hi"`, then `"Hello to you too!"` is displayed. This matches `"hello"` because there is no `break` after that test and execution 'trickles down' until it is stopped by the first `break` :

```
case "hello":
case "hi":
    output.Text = "Hello to you too!";
    break;
```

If `userinput.Text` is anything else, the code in the `default` section is run, so `"I don't understand that!"` is displayed:

```
default:
    output.Text = "I don't understand that!";
    break;
```

Operators

Operators are special symbols that are used to do specific operations such as the addition and subtraction of numbers or the concatenation (adding together) of strings.

Assignment Operator

One of the most important operators is the assignment operator, `=`, which assigns the value on its right to a variable on its left. Note that the type of data assigned must be compatible with the type of the variable. This assigns an integer value (`10`) to an `int` variable, `myintvariable`:

```
int myintvariable = 10;
```

Arithmetic Operators

I've already used some arithmetic operators in previous programs – for example, in the tax calculator (Chapter 2) I calculated values by adding and subtracting numbers using the addition `+` and subtraction `-` operators. The other operators you need to know are the division `/` and multiplication `*` operators which divide and multiply one value by the other and the remainder (or 'modulus') operator `%` which calculates the remainder after a division. Here are some examples of these operators:

```
100 + 7
100 - 7
100 / 7
100 % 7
```

Here you can see how I have used these operators in program code:

ArithmeticOps

```
textBox1.AppendText("100 + 7=" + (100 + 7) + "\r\n");
textBox1.AppendText("100 - 7=" + (100 - 7) + "\r\n");
textBox1.AppendText("100 * 7=" + (100 * 7) + "\r\n");
textBox1.AppendText("100 / 7=" + (100 / 7) + "\r\n");
textBox1.AppendText("100 % 7=" + (100 % 7) + "\r\n");
```

This program produces this output:

```
100 + 7=107
100 - 7=93
100 * 7=700
100 / 7=14
100 % 7=2
```

The String Concatenation Operator

Bear in mind that the `+` operator is used not only to add numbers but also to concatenate strings. C# works out whether the `+` operator adds or concatenates based on the context.

If `+` is placed between two strings, then it is obviously a concatenation operator. If it's between two numbers, then it's an addition operator. But what about if it's between a string and a number as in this code?

```
textBox1.AppendText("Result =" + 100 + "\r\n");
```

In this case, C# assumes you want to concatenate the string representation of the number to the string before the `+` operator. It therefore automatically converts the number 100 to the string `"100"` before adding it onto the end of the string `"Result ="`. So the output from the above code would be the string:

```
"Result = 100"
```

Be careful though. Look at this:

```
textBox1.AppendText("155 + 3=" + 155 + 3 + "\r\n");
```

You might assume that here the integer 155 will be added to 3 and the result, 158, will be converted to the string `"158"` and that this string will then be concatenated onto the string `"155 + 3="`. In fact, that's *not* what happens.

What actually happens is that 155 is converted to a string, `"155"`, 3 is converted to a string `"3"` and those two strings are then concatenated onto the preceding string, so that this is the output:

```
155 + 3=1553
```

If you want the + between the two integers to be treated as an arithmetic operator, you should put the complete arithmetic expression inside parentheses like this:

ArithmeticOps

```
textBox1.AppendText("155+3=" + (155 + 3) + "\r\n");
```

This ensures that the addition operation is evaluated as a single unit and the result, 158, will then be converted to a string and concatenated onto the preceding string. Now, this is what will be displayed when the string is appended to the text box:

```
155 + 3=158
```

This is one more example of how the addition of a simple pair of parentheses can ensure that your code does what you intend it to do!

Comparison Operators

These are the most common comparison operators that you will use in tests:

```
==      // equals
!=      // not equals
>       // greater than
<       // less than
<=      // less than or equal to
>=      // greater than or equal to
```

These operators are placed between two values, inside parentheses, to test one value against the other. For example, this is how I would test if `value1` is *less than* `value2`. If it is, then any code between { and } would be executed:

```
if (value1 < value2) { // some code }
```

Similarly, I could test if `value1` is *greater than* `value2`:

```
if (value1 > value2) { // some code }
```

The code shown below tests if the value of `i` is less than *or equal to* the value of `j`. If it is, then the test evaluates to `true` and `"Test is true"` is displayed. Otherwise the test evaluates to `false` and `"Test is false"` is displayed:

Tests

```
int i = 100;
int j = 200;
if(i <= j) {
    output.Text = "Test is true";
} else {
    output.Text = "Test is false";
}
```

Since, in this case, `i` (100) is less than or equal to `j` (200), this is displayed:

```
Test is true
```

You can change the test shown above by substituting different comparison operators. For example, this test returns `true` if the value of `i` is equal to the value of `j`:

```
if(i == j)
```

And this test returns `true` if the value of `i` is *not equal to* the value of `j`:

```
if(i != j)
```

= or == ?

While one equals sign = is used to assign a value, two equals signs, ==, are used to test a condition.

= The assignment operator. This assigns 1 to the variable x:

```
x = 1;                          // assignment
```

== The equality operator. This tests if x has the value 1:

```
if (x == 1)                     // test for equality
```

Logical Operators

In some of the code examples in this chapter, I have used the `&&` operator to mean 'and' and the `||` operator to mean 'or'. You'll find this example in the *Tests* project:

Tests

```
if((msglen == 0) && (namelen == 0)) {
    output.Text = "You haven't entered anything!";
} else if((msglen == 0) || (namelen == 0)) {
    output.Text = "You must enter something into both text boxes";
} else if((msg != "hi") && (msg != "hello")) {
    output.Text = "Please enter a friendly greeting ('hi' or 'hello')";
} else {
    output.Text = "Well, " + msg + " to you too, " + name;
}
```

The `&&` and `||` operators are called 'logical operators'. Logical operators can help you chain together conditions when you want to take some action only when *all* of a set of conditions are true or when *any one* of a set of conditions is true. For example, you might want to offer a discount to customers only when they have bought goods worth more than 100 dollars *and* they have also bought the deal of the day. In code these conditions could be evaluated using the logical *and* (`&&`) operator, like this:

```
if ((valueOfPurchases > 100) && (boughtDealOfTheDay))
```

But if you are feeling more generous, you might want to offer a discount *either* if a customer has bought goods worth more than 100 dollars *or* has bought the deal of the day. In code these conditions can be evaluated using the logical *or* (`||`) operator, like this:

```
if ((valueOfPurchases > 100) || (boughtDealOfTheDay))
```

- When a test includes multiple parts or 'conditions', each condition enclosed by a pair of parentheses can evaluate to `true` or `false`.
- When multiple conditions are separated by `&&` ('and') operators *all* those conditions must evaluate to `true` in order for the entire test to evaluate to `true`.
- When multiple conditions are separated by `||` ('or') operators *any one* of those conditions must evaluate to `true` in order for the entire test to evaluate to `true`.

Short-circuit Operators

One aspect of the logical operators && and || that is not obvious at first sight is that they are 'short-circuit' or 'minimal evaluation' operators. This means that the first part of the expression is enough to determine whether the action should be performed. So look at this example:

```
int x = 1, y = 2;
if ((x == 1) && (y == 2)) { ... }
```

The test (y == 2) will not be performed even though it would succeed – the test is said to be 'short-circuited'. Now look at this code:

```
string str = "hello";
if ((str != null) && (str.Length > 0)) {... }
```

Again, no problem: str is not null and all is well. Finally, look at this:

```
string str = null;
if ((str != null) && (str.Length > 0)) {... }
```

The short-circuiting effect will stop an exception being thrown by the second test (s.Length > 0) because str is null. The first test evaluates to false, so it doesn't matter what the result of the second test is – the action will not be performed. But the second test is not evaluated – because && is a short-circuit operator. But what if the test were the other way round?

```
string str = null;
if ((str.Length > 0) && (str != null)) {// oops! crash!! ... }
```

In this case, an exception will be thrown because str is null and trying to get the length of a null string pointer is not allowed.

! The Logical Not Operator

Just as the test for equality can be negated using the not-equals operator != instead of the equals operator ==, so too other tests can be negated by preceding the test with a single exclamation mark ! which is called the 'logical not operator'. So if age is less than or equal to 30 and salary is greater than or equal to 30000.00, this test succeeds:

```
if ((age <= 30) && (salary >= 30000.00)) {
```

But this test fails (due to the !), fails:

```
if (!((age <= 30) && (salary >= 30000.00))) {
```

You will find some examples of using these operators in the *LogicalOperators* sample program (shown on the next page). Notice that, once again, when a test involves multiple test conditions, I place each test condition between a pair of parentheses. As I mentioned earlier, this is not always strictly necessary and experienced programmers (assuming they know all the rules of operator precedence) may prefer to use fewer parentheses. However, parentheses often help to resolve any possible ambiguities in your code. When run, the *LogicalOperators* program produces this output:

```
You are not a rich young person
You are either rich or young or both
You are not a rich young parent
```

Operator precedence

If you don't put test conditions between parentheses, C# will evaluate the elements of a test in a predefined order, so some operators will always cause expressions to be evaluated before other operators. The default order of evaluation is described as 'operator precedence'. This is explained in more detail in the Microsoft document:

https://msdn.microsoft.com/en-us/library/2bxt6kc4.aspx

Making mistakes by assuming an incorrect operator precedence can cause your code to behave incorrectly. Many of these sorts of mistake can be avoided by placing conditions between pairs of parentheses to force them to be evaluated as a single test.

LogicalOperators

```
int age;
int number_of_children;
double salary;
double bonus;

age = 25;
number_of_children = 1;
salary = 20000.00;
bonus = 500.00;

if ((age <= 30) && (salary >= 30000.00)) {
    textBox1.AppendText("You are a rich young person\r\n");
} else {
    textBox1.AppendText("You are not a rich young person\r\n");
}

// Negate this test with a !
if (!((age <= 30) && (salary >= 30000.00))) {
    textBox1.AppendText("You are a rich young person\r\n");
} else {
    textBox1.AppendText("You are not a rich young person\r\n");
}

if ((age <= 30) || (salary >= 30000.00)) {
    textBox1.AppendText("You are either rich or young or both\r\n");
} else {
    textBox1.AppendText("You are not neither rich nor young\r\n");
}

if ((age <= 30) && (salary >= 30000.00) && (number_of_children != 0)) {
    textBox1.AppendText("You are a rich young parent\r\n");
} else {
    textBox1.AppendText("You are not a rich young parent\r\n");
}
```

Try changing some of the operators to understand how they work. For example, I could change the `&&` to `||` in the last `if` test like this:

```
if ((age <= 30) || (salary >= 30000.00) && (number_of_children != 0))
```

The output now shows that the test succeeds when previously it failed:

```
You are a rich young parent
```

That's because the test no longer requires that *all* conditions are met – only that *either* the first conditions *or* the last two conditions are met.

Keep it simple!

As a rule, try not to have too many conditions linked with && and || as the more complex the conditions become the more likely you are to make a mistake of logic that could result in hard-to-find program bugs.

When Tests Are Too Complex

Let me give you an example a confusing test condition. Take a look at this code:

LogicalOperators

```
age = 25;
number_of_children = 1;
salary = 20000.00;
bonus = 500.00;

if (age > 20 && salary > 10000.00 || number_of_children == 1 && bonus > 8000.00){
   textBox1.AppendText("You've won the star prize!");
} else {
    textBox1.AppendText("Sorry, you are not a winner\n");
}
```

Can you work out which of the two specified strings will actually be printed out? If you can't figure it out right away, that's not surprising. Because the test is too complicated. Let's run it and see. This is what it shows:

```
"You've won the star prize!"
```

Does it mean that there are *two* necessary conditions of winning? Namely:

1 that your age is greater than twenty **AND** your salary is greater than 10,0000 – **OR**, alternatively, that you have one child …

… ***and also***:

2 that your bonus must be greater than 8000?

If that is what you intend, then this is the *first* condition:

```
age > 20 && salary > 10000.00 || number_of_children == 1
```

And here's the *second* condition:

```
bonus > 800.00
```

We can clarify this by putting parentheses around the separate conditions like this so that condition [1] above is now enclosed within a pair of parentheses:

```
(age > 20 && salary > 10000.00) || number_of_children == 1)
```

This is how the test would now be written:

```
if((age > 20 && salary > 10000.00) || number_of_children == 1) && bonus > 800.00)
```

Now this is the output:

```
"Sorry, you are not a winner"
```

So how does a single pair of parentheses change the results of the test? Let's see what's going on here. In my original code, without the conditions placed between parentheses, the test was evaluated according to the rules of operator precedence.

As I said earlier, operator precedence can be quite hard to understand, especially in a test such as the one above that includes both *logical* (`&&` and `||`) and *comparison* (`>` and `==`) operators.

By adding parentheses to ensure that a particular set of conditions is evaluated as a single '*sub-test*' (which returns `true` or `false`), I have changed how the *entire* test is evaluated. You could try adding parentheses around different parts of this test to see how the end result may change.

The lesson to be learnt here is that the test itself is too complicated. It is simply too hard to understand what exactly it all means just by looking at the code. If you plan to use test conditions, try to keep them as simple as possible! If they can't be kept simple, consider grouping together any bits of the test that should be evaluated together by placing them between parentheses.

Simplifying Complex Tests

There are many possible ways of avoiding over-complex test conditions. You could, for example, use `if` and `else` tests to divide a long test condition into a sequence of smaller and simpler tests. In some cases, a `switch` statement might be a good choice.

Compound Assignment Operators

Some assignment operators in C#, and other C-like languages, perform a calculation prior to assigning the result to a variable. These are called 'compound assignment operators'.

Here are some examples of common compound assignment operators along with the non-compound equivalent.

operator	example	equivalent to
`+=`	`a += b`	`a = a + b`
`-=`	`a -= b`	`a = a - b`
`*=`	`a *= b`	`a = a * b`
`/=`	`a /= b`	`a = a / b`

It is up to you which syntax you prefer to use in your own code. If you are familiar with other C-like languages, you may already have a preference. Java, C and C++ programmers may prefer the short form as in `a += b`. Basic and Pascal programmers may feel more comfortable with the slightly longer form as in `a = a + b`. Here are a few examples from the *Operators* project:

Operators

```
int a = 10;
int b = 2;
tb.Clear();
AddToTextBox("a + b     : " + (a + b));
AddToTextBox("a = " + a);
AddToTextBox("a += b  : " + (a += b));
AddToTextBox("a = " + a);
AddToTextBox("a - b     : " + (a - b));
AddToTextBox("a = " + a);
AddToTextBox("a -= b  : " + (a -= b));
AddToTextBox("a = " + a);
AddToTextBox("a * b     : " + (a * b));
```

Operators (continued)

```
AddToTextBox("a = " + a);
AddToTextBox("a *= b  : " + (a *= b));
AddToTextBox("a = " + a);
AddToTextBox("a / b     : " + (a / b));
AddToTextBox("a = " + a);
AddToTextBox("a /= b  : " + (a /= b));
AddToTextBox("a = " + a);
```

This is what appears in the text box (note how the value of a changes after compound assignment operators but not when an operation is performed without assignment):

```
a + b   : 12
a = 10
a += b  : 12
a = 12
a - b   : 10
a = 12
a -= b  : 10
a = 10
a * b   : 20
a = 10
a *= b  : 20
a = 20
a / b   : 10
a = 20
a /= b  : 10
a = 10
```

Increment ++ and Decrement -- Operators

When you want to increment (add to) or decrement (subtract from) the value of a variable by 1, you may use the ++ and -- operators. Here is an example of the increment (++) operator:

```
int num = 100;
num++;  // num is now 101

int num = 100;
num--;  // num is now 99
```

Unary operators

++ and -- are called 'unary operators' because they only require one value, one 'operand', to work upon (e.g. a++) whereas binary operators such as + and - require two (e.g. a + b).

Prefix and Postfix Operators

You may place the ++ and -- operators either before or after a variable like this: a++ or like this: ++a. Typically, this is done when you want to increment a variable and assign its value. When one of these operators is placed *before* a variable, the value of that variable is incremented or decremented before any assignment is made:

Operators

```
int a;
a = 10;
b = ++a;          // both a and b equal 11
```

After this code executes, a has the value 11; and b also has the value 11. However, when the operator is placed *after* a variable, the assignment of the existing value is done *before* the variable's value is incremented:

```
int a;
a = 10;
b = a++;          // a equals 11, but b equals 10
```

After the above code executes, a has the value 11; but b has the value 10.

Prefix or Postfix?

Mixing prefix and postfix operators in your code can be confusing and may lead to hard-to-find bugs. It is to your advantage, whenever possible, to keep things simple and clear by only ever using one or the other .In fact, there is nothing wrong with using the longer form by doing an explicit arithmetical operation and then assigning the result. This may seem more verbose but it is at least completely unambiguous:

```
b = a + 1;
b = a - 1;
```

4 – Functions

Functions provide ways of dividing your code into named 'chunks'. In this chapter I explain how to write functions, pass arguments to them and return a value from a function.

A function is a named block of code. A function is declared using a keyword such as `private` or `public` (which controls the degree of visibility of the function to the rest of the code in the program) followed by the data type of any value that's returned by the function or `void` if nothing is returned. Then comes the name of the function, which may be chosen by the programmer. Then comes a pair of parentheses.

Using Functions

Here is a function called `ShowMessage()`. It is `private`, which means it is only visible to code inside the current class (in the sample program that happens to be `Form1`, the class that defines the main form of the application), it takes a single string argument, `aMessage`, and it turns nothing (`void`):

Methods

```
private void ShowMessage( string aMessage ) {
    // some code goes here…
}
```

Access Modifiers

Keywords that affect the 'visibility' of functions, such as `private` and `public` are called 'access modifiers'. We'll see them again in Chapter 5.

When a function is declared, its parentheses may contain zero or more 'parameters' separated by commas. The parameters represent pieces of data that have been passed to the function. The parameter names are chosen by the programmer and each parameter must be preceded by its data type. When a function returns some value to the code that called it, that return value is indicated by preceding it with the `return` keyword.

In C#, the word 'method' is often used to describe a function. 'Method' is the object-oriented term for a function that is bound into an object. The idea is that your code may pass a 'message' to an object (when it calls a function) and the object looks for some 'method' of responding to that message. If you find this idea odd or confusing, don't worry. It is sufficient to know that in an object-oriented language such as C#, the words 'function' and 'method' are used more or less interchangeably. I'll have more to say about object orientation in the next chapter.

Parameters and Arguments

Parameters are the variables declared between parentheses in the function itself, like this:

```
private string AddNumbers(int num1, int num2)
```

Arguments are the values passed to the function when that function is called, like this:

```
AddNumbers(100, 200);
```

Arguments or Parameters?

While computer scientists may like to make a clear distinction between the terms 'parameter' and 'argument', computer programmers are often less precise. Informally, a function's 'parameter list' is often referred to as its 'argument list'.

When you call a function, you must pass to it the same number of arguments as the parameters declared by the function. Each argument in the list must be of the same data type as the matching parameter. If more than one argument is expected, the parameters must be separated by commas. If no arguments are expected, an empty pair of parentheses must be placed after the function name. Here are some example functions.

A function that takes no arguments and returns nothing (`void`):

Methods

```
private void SayHello() {
    textBox1.AppendText("Hello\r\n");
}
```

A function that takes a single argument of the `string` data-type and returns nothing:

```
private void Greet(string aName) {
    textBox1.AppendText("Hello, " + aName + "\r\n");
}
```

A function that takes two arguments of the `int` data-type and returns a `string`:

```
private string AddNumbers(int num1, int num2) {
    return "The total of " + num1 + " plus " + num2 + " is " + num1 + num2;
}
```

Calling Functions

To execute the code in a function, your code must 'call' the function by name. In C#, to call a function with no arguments, you must enter the function name followed by an empty pair of parentheses like this:

```
SayHello();
```

To call a function with a single argument, you must enter the function name followed by a single value or variable of the correct data type (to match the corresponding parameter that has been declared by the function), like this:

```
Greet("Mary");
Add10(100);
```

To call a function with more than one argument, you must enter the function name followed by the correct number and data-type of values or variables, like this:

```
AddNumbers(100, 200);
```

If a function returns a value, that value may be assigned (in the calling code) to a variable of the matching data-type. Here, `AddNumbers()` function returns a string:

```
string calcResult;
calcResult = AddNumbers(100, 200);
```

Here, two integers are passed to the `Add()` function which returns an integer. The returned integer value is assigned to the `total` variable:

```
int total;
total = Add(60, 12);
```

Parameters Must Match Arguments

I said earlier that arguments passed to a function must match the corresponding parameters declared by the function in both number and type. If a function declares three `string` parameters and two `int` parameters then, when that function is called, three strings and two integers must be passed to it. These may be actual (literal) strings and integers such as `"Mary"` and `100` or they may be `string` and `int` variables to which strings and integers have been assigned.

Similarly, if a function returns a value, that value can be assigned to a variable of the same type. Alternatively, the return value may be passed directly to another function as an argument. This is done by placing the first function-call inside the pair of parentheses of the second function-call. This annotated code snippet illustrates this:

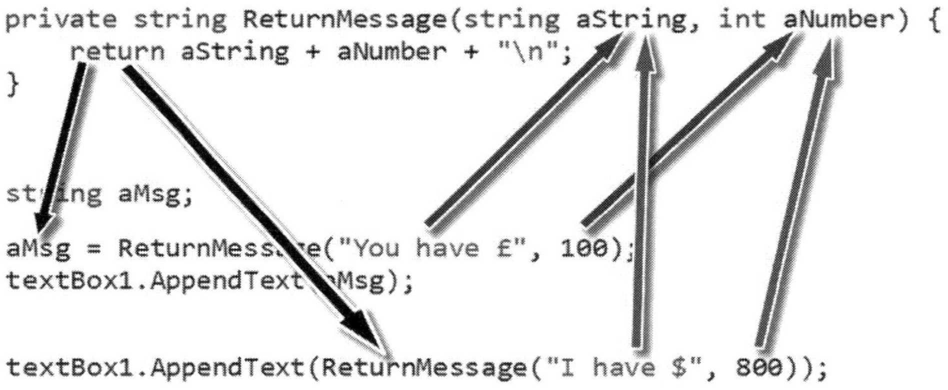

Here, the `ReturnMessage()` function declares a `string` parameter, `aString`, and an `int` parameter, `aNumber`. When I call that function, I must call it with one string and one integer argument. The string argument (such as `"You have £"`) is assigned to the matching `string` parameter, `aString`. The integer argument (such as `100`) is assigned to the matching `int` argument, `aNumber`.

The `ReturnMessage()` function returns a `string` value. This may be assigned to a `string` variable, such as `aMsg`. Alternatively, the returned value may be passed directly (without assigning it to a variable) to some other function that expects a `string` argument. That is what I have done in the final line of code:

```
textBox1.AppendText(ReturnMessage("I have $", 800));
```

Value, Reference and Out Parameters

By default, when you pass variables to functions or methods these are passed as 'copies'. That is, their values are passed as arguments and these values are assigned to the corresponding parameters declared by the function. Any changes made within the method will affect only the copies (the parameters) within the scope of the method. The original variables that were passed as arguments (and which were declared outside the method) retain their original values.

Methods

Remember, 'method' is just the object oriented name for a function that is bound into an object. From now on, I will often refer to C# functions as 'methods'.

Sometimes, however, you may in fact want any changes that are made to parameters inside a method to change the matching variables (the arguments) in the code that called the method. In order to do that, you can pass variables 'by reference'. When variables are passed by reference, the original variables (or, to be more accurate, the references to the location of those variables in your computer's memory) are passed to the function. So any changes made to the parameter values inside the function will also change the variables that were passed as arguments when the function was called.

To pass arguments *by reference*, both the parameters defined by the function *and* the arguments passed to the function must be preceded by the keyword `ref`. The following examples should clarify the difference between 'by value' and a 'by reference' arguments. In each case, I assume that two `int` variables have been declared like this:

```
int firstnumber;
int secondnumber;
firstnumber = 10;
secondnumber = 20;
```

Example 1: By Value Parameters

```
Methods
private void ByValue(int num1, int num2) {
    num1 = 0;
    num2 = 1;
}
```

This method might be called like this:

```
ByValue(firstnumber, secondnumber);
```

Remember that `firstnumber` had the initial value of 10, and `secondnumber` had the initial value of 20. Only the *copies* (the values of the parameters, `num1` and `num2`) were changed in the `ByValue()` method. So, after I call that method, the values of the two variables that I passed as arguments are unchanged:

> `firstnumber` now has the value 10.
> `secondnumber` now has the value 20.

Example 2: By Reference Parameters

```
Methods
private void ByReference(ref int num1, ref int num2) {
    num1 = 0;
    num2 = 1;
}
```

This method might be called like this:

```
ByReference(ref firstnumber, ref secondnumber);
```

Once again, `firstnumber` has the initial value of 10, and `secondnumber` has the initial value of 20. But these are now `ref` parameters, so the parameters `num1` and `num2` 'refer' to the original variables. When changes are made to the parameters, the original variables are also changed:

> `firstnumber` now has the value 0.
> `secondnumber` now has the value 1.

You may also use *out* parameters which must be preceded by the `out` keyword instead of the `ref` keyword.

Example 3: out Parameters

```
private void OutParams(out int num1, out int num2) {
    num1 = 0;
    num2 = 1;
}
```

This method might be called like this:

```
int firstnumber;
int secondnumber;
OutParams(out firstnumber, out secondnumber);
```

In this case, as with ref parameters, the vales of the variables that were passed as arguments are changed when the values of the parameters are changed:

> `firstnumber` now has the value 0.
> `secondnumber` now has the value 1.

At first sight, `out` parameters may seem similar to `ref` parameters. However, it is *not* obligatory to assign a value to a variable passed as an `out` argument *before* you pass it to a method. It *is* obligatory to assign a value to a variable passed as a `ref` argument.

You can see this in the example shown above. I *do not* initialize the values of `firstnumber` and `secondnumber` before calling the `OutParams()` method. That would not be permitted if I were using ordinary (by value) or `ref` (by reference) parameters. On the other hand, it is obligatory to assign a value to an `out` parameter *within* the method that declares that parameter. This is not obligatory with a `ref` argument.

Which Parameters Are Best?

You need to recognise `ref` and `out` arguments when you see them. Even so, you may not have any compelling reason to use them in your own programs. There are some cases when they are useful. However, I would suggest that you generally use the default 'by value' arguments for C# unless you have a good reason for using one of the other types of argument.

Local Functions

You can also write 'local functions' – that is, functions that are written inside other functions. Local functions may be useful when you need to do some operation repeatedly within the context of some other function but nowhere else in your code. In the code show below, AddBonus() is a local function:

LocalFunctions

```
private string ShowSalary(string aName, int earnings) {
string msg;
double bonus;

    double AddBonus() {
        return earnings + (earnings * 0.05);
    }

   bonus = AddBonus();
   msg = aName + " has a salary of " + bonus + "\r\n";
    return msg;
}
```

In this example, the AddBonus() function is 'local' to the ShowSalary() function because it is declared inside that function. The AddBonus() function returns a double value. Notice that I haven't used the keyword public or private with this local function as I would with a regular function. That's because those keywords define the visibility or 'scope' of a function. The scope of AddBonus() is already defined. It is only visible inside the ShowSalary() function. That means that only the code in the ShowSalary() function is able to 'see' and, therefore, to call the AddBonus() function, as I have done here:

```
double AddBonus() {
    return earnings + (earnings * 0.05);
}

bonus = AddBonus();
```

The AddBonus() function can access the variables or parameters defined within its own scope – in other words, any variables or parameters available inside the ShowSalary() function. In the code fragment shown above, you can see that AddBonus() accesses the earnings parameter which was declared by the ShowSalary() function:

```
private string ShowSalary(string aName, int earnings)
```

5 – Object Orientation

C# is an Object Oriented Programming (OOP) language. In this chapter I explain how to write your own classes and create objects from them.

Everything you work with in C# – from a string such as `"Hello world"` to a file on disk – is wrapped up inside an object that contains the data itself (for example, the characters in a string) and the functions or 'methods' that can be used to manipulate that data – such as, for example, the `ToUpper()` method, which returns the string in upper case.

Object Orientation

Each object that you use is created from a 'class'. You can think of a class as a blueprint that defines the structure (the data) and the behaviour (the methods) of an object. Let's look at an example of a very simple class definition:

MyOb

```
class MyClass {
    private string _s;

    public MyClass() {
        _s = "Hello world";
    }

    public string GetS() {
        return _s;
    }

    public void SetS(string aString) {
        _s = aString;
    }
}
```

You define a class using the `class` keyword. Here I have decided to call the class `MyClass`. It contains a string, `_s`. I've made this string '`private`' which means that code outside the class is unable to access the string variable. In order to access the string any code outside the class use the methods which I've written – `GetS()` and `SetS()`. It is generally good practice to make variables `private`. By using methods to access variables you are able to test that data is valid (before assigning or returning values) and control how much access is permitted to the variables inside an object. A method could, for example, restrict the amount of currency that can be returned from an internal variable called `some_money` whereas if that variable were `public`, and so could be accessed directly, the user would be able to withdraw any amount of currency with no limit.

At this point, the `MyClass` class doesn't actually do anything. It is simply a definition or 'blueprint' for objects which don't yet exist. In the *MyOb* project, I declare an object variable of the `MyClass` type:

```
MyClass ob;
```

But before I can use the object, I need to create it. I do that by using the `new` keyword. This calls the `MyClass` constructor method and that returns a new `MyClass` object which I here assign to the `ob` variable:

```
ob = new MyClass();
```

Constructors

A constructor is a special method which, in C#, has the same name as the class itself. This is the `MyClass` constructor:

MyOb

```
public MyClass() {
    _s = "Hello world";
}
```

The code in this constructor assigns the string `"Hello world"` to the variable `_s`. You aren't obliged to write any code in a constructor. However, it is quite common – and good practice – to assign default values to an object's 'fields' or variables in the constructor. I have also written a `SetS()` method:

```
public void SetS(string aString) {
    _s = aString;
}
```

You can call `SetS()` when you want to change the default value of each object's `_s` string variable:

```
ob.SetS("A new string");
```

And you can retrieve the value of the `_s` variable using the `GetS()` method:

```
textBox1.Text = ob.GetS();
```

Classes, Objects and Methods

Let's quickly summarise the essential details of classes, objects and methods. A '**class**' is the blueprint for an object. It defines the data an object contains and the way it behaves. This is the blueprint of a car:

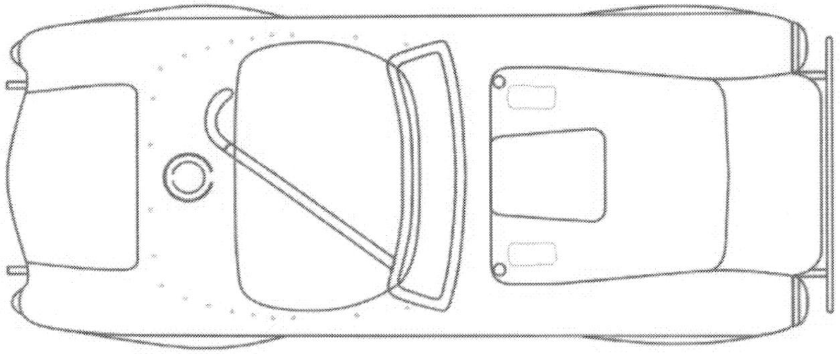

This is a very simple C# class to define a `Car`:

Cars

```
class Car {
    private string _name;
    private int _speed;
}
```

In the real world, you can't drive the blueprint of a car. Someone has to construct a car (a car '**object**') based on the blueprint. In the Object Orientated world, you can't use my `Car` class until you construct a `Car` object based on the class.

Whenever a new `Car` object is constructed, it needs to be assigned a name and a speed. In C#, I do that in a special 'constructor' method that has the same name as the class. Let's add a constructor method to my `Car` class:

```
class Car {
    private string _name;
    private int _speed;

    public Car() {
        _name = "Generic Car\r\n";
        _speed = 0;
    }
}
```

The constructor assigns default values to the private fields of each newly constructed `Car` object. I can now construct numerous different `Car` objects by calling the constructor after the `new` keyword then assigning the `Car` object to a `Car` variable:

```
Car car1;
Car car2;
Car car3;

car1 = new Car();
car2 = new Car();
car3 = new Car();
```

This is the programmatic equivalent of constructing three cars from one blueprint:

Having constructed some `Car` objects, I now want to change their default names and speeds. I can do that using methods. A '**method**' is a function or subroutine that is defined inside the class. These are my methods to change (get or set) the speed of a `Car` object:

```
public int GetSpeed() {
    return _speed;
}

public void SetSpeed(int aSpeed) {
    _speed = aSpeed;
}
```

I can call a method by writing the name of an object, followed by a dot, the name of a method and a pair of parentheses (with any arguments) and a semicolon, like this:

```
car1.SetSpeed(80);
car2.SetSpeed(120);
car3.SetSpeed(100);
```

You can find this code in the *Cars* sample project.

null objects

If you try to use an object before it has been created, C# throws an exception (an error). In the *Cars* project, if you click the button to show the cars before you have created any car objects, your program will crash with a '`NullReferenceException`'. I'll explain how to deal with exceptions in Chapter 9. For now, in order to avoid this problem, my code checks if any of my three car objects is `null`; in C#, `null` is a special value that indicates that an object variable does not refer to an actual object (because the object has not yet been constructed). The code that calls the `Car` methods only executes if none of the car objects is `null`:

```
if (car1 == null || car2 == null || car3 == null) {
    textBox1.Text = " No cars have been constructed!\r\n";
} else {
    textBox1.AppendText(car1.Description());
    textBox1.AppendText(car2.Description());
    textBox1.AppendText(car3.Description());
}
```

Inheritance

Inheritance is one of the key features of object orientation. The idea is that you create a simple class and then you define more specialised classes that inherit all the features of that class and add on additional features of their own. That means you don't have to re-code the same features over and over again. Features of 'ancestor' classes are automatically 'inherited' by descendant classes.

For example, you could create a 'family tree' of `Car` classes. A `SportsCar` might inherit all the features of a `Car` but add on two extra features: `TurboThruster` and `GoFasterStripe`. Another class called `LuxuryCar` might also descend from the `Car` class. It would add on the extra features: `DeluxeUpholstery` and `IntegralCocktailCabinet`.

Class Hierarchies

To create a descendant of a class, put a colon : plus the ancestor (or 'base') class name after the name of the descendant class, like this:

```
public class Treasure : Thing
```

A descendant class inherits the features (the methods and variables) of its ancestor so you don't need to recode them. Look at the `Thing` and `Treasure` classes which you'll find in the code file *GameClasses.cs* in the *GameClasses* project, (shown on the next page).

Here the `Thing` class has two private variables, `_name` and `_description` (being private they cannot be accessed from outside the class) and two public properties, `Name` and `Description`, to access those variables.

Properties – a first look

Here `Name` and `Description` are 'properties'. These provide a convenient way of accessing variables in an object. Properties are explained later in this chapter.

The `Treasure` class is a descendant of the `Thing` class so it automatically has the `_name` and `_description` variables (it 'inherits' them from its ancestor class, `Thing`) and also the `Name` and `Description` properties; it adds on the `_value` variable and the `Value` property.

GameClasses (GameClasses.cs)

```
public class Thing {
    private string _name;
    private string _description;

    public Thing(string aName, string aDescription) {
        _name = aName;
        _description = aDescription;
    }

    public string Name {
        get {
            return _name;
        }
        set {
            _name = value;
        }
    }

    public string Description {
        get {
            return _description;
        }
        set {
            _description = value;
        }
    }
}

public class Treasure : Thing {
    private double _value;

    public Treasure(string aName, string aDescription, double aValue)
        : base(aName, aDescription) {
        _value = aValue;
    }

    public double Value {
        get {
            return _value;
        }
        set {
            _value = value;
        }
    }
}
```

In fact, my *GameClasses* project also creates another descendant of `Thing`. The `Room` class also inherits `Name` and `Description`. It adds on four direction properties (and variables):

```
public Room(string aName, string aDescription, int aN, int aS, int aW, int anE)
    : base(aName, aDescription) {
    _n = aN;
    _s = aS;
    _w = aW;
    _e = anE;
}

public int N {
    get {
        return _n;
    }
    set {
        _n = value;
    }
}

public int S {
    get {
        return _s;
    }
    set {
        _s = value;
    }
}

public int W {
    get {
        return _w;
    }
    set {
        _w = value;
    }
}


public int E {
    get {
        return _e;
    }
    set {
        _e = value;
    }
}
```

Notice that, in order to initialize the data of its 'superclass' (that is, its immediate ancestor) both `Treasure` and `Room` need to pass the arguments required by the `Thing` constructor method. Here these are the `aName` and `aDescription` arguments. They are passed to the constructor of the superclass using the `base` keyword after the parameter list of the descendant class's constructor, followed by a colon:

```
public Treasure(string aName, string aDescription, double aValue)
: base(aName, aDescription)
```

```
public Room(string aName, string aDescription, int aN, int aS, int aW, int anE)
: base(aName, aDescription)
```

This diagram represents my 'class hierarchy' with the `Treasure` and `Room` classes both descending from the `Thing` class and inheriting `Name` and `Description`. `Treasure` adds `Value`. Room adds `N`, `S`, `W` and `E`:

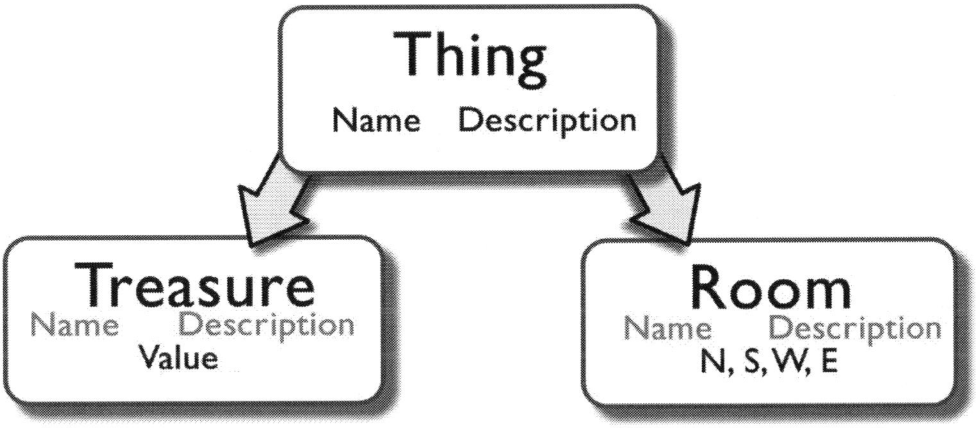

You aren't restricted to just one 'level' of inheritance. I could go on to add subclasses of `Room` and `Treasure`. For example, I could create a `Weapon` class that descends from `Treasure`. The `Weapon` class would inherit all the features of its superclass (`Treasure`) and of all other ancestors (here its only other ancestor is `Thing`). It would *not* inherit features from classes that are not its ancestors though (such as `Room`). So if I create a `Weapon` class that descends from `Treasure` it would inherit `Name`, `Description` and `Value`. I could then add extra features that are specific to `Weapon` objects – such as `DestructivePower`. You may want to try extending the code in the *GameClasses* project to see if you can create a `Weapon` class.

An object is an 'instance' of a class

In object oriented terminology, the word 'instance' is sometimes used to describe an object. Variables and methods that 'belong' to an object may be called 'instance variables' and 'instance methods'.

One Class Per Code File?

In C#, you may define several different classes in a single code file. For example, the `Thing`, `Treasure` and `Room` classes might all be defined (as I have done) in a file called *GameClasses.cs*. However, many programmers consider it better to define just one class per code file. In large projects this may make it easier to find and maintain the classes you create. In that case, the `Thing` class would be defined in a file called *Thing.cs*, the `Treasure` class would be defined in *Treasure.cs* and the `Room` class would be defined in *Room.cs*. This is what I will do when I return to this simple game project in Chapter 10.

Refactoring

Visual Studio has a refactoring tool to help you to extract classes from a code file containing several classes and put them into separate code files. Right-click a class name (e.g. `Treasure`), select *Quick Actions and Refactorings*, then *Move Type To...* In this case, this would move the definition of the `Treasure` class into a code file named *Treasure.cs*.

Access Modifiers

We've seen the keywords `private` and `public` many times in my code examples. When placed before an identifier such as the declaration of a variable or function, these limit the scope or visibility of that variable or function.

public and private

A `public` variable or function can be 'seen', and therefore accessed, from code outside the object in which it occurs; a `private` variable or function cannot. Typically you will make variables `private` and provide `public` accessor methods when you want to get and set their values.

When you want a method to be callable from any code that uses an object, you will declare it as `public`. If, for some reason, you want a method to be callable only from other methods inside an object, then you will normally make that `private`.

protected

There is another access modifier that you may occasionally encounter called `protected`. A `protected` variable or method can only be accessed from within inside the class in which it is declared or from inside any *descendant* of that class. That's different from a `private` variable or method which can be accessed only from inside the *current* class but *not* from inside one of its *descendant* classes.

While `protected` variables and methods are sometimes useful, the two most common accessor levels are `public` and `private`. It is good practice to make the variables or 'fields' of objects `private`.

Example: public, private, protected

The *Scope* project, shown on the next page, uses accessor modifiers with variables. These modifiers would have the same effect if used with methods. This example illustrates, in some detail, the differences between `public`, `private` and `protected`. If you don't plan to use `protected` in your own code, you can skip this section for now.

In this example, class `B` is a descendant of class `A`. Class `A` declares three variables, `x`, `y` and `z`. Its constructor gives each variable a default value whenever a new object is created. When `button1` is clicked, the code in `button1_Click()` creates the `b` object which is an instance of class `B`.

Within the scope of the `Form1` class, I try to display the values of each of the three variables by accessing them from the `B` object (`b.x`, `b.y`, `b.z`). Remember that these variables are all declared and initialized in class `A` which is the ancestor class of `B`.

The variable `x` is no problem. It's `public` so it's visible just about everywhere.

```
textBox1.AppendText("b.x=" + b.x + "\r\n");
```

I can't get at the variable `y` though because it's `private`. That means it's only visible to code *inside* the `A` class. As a result, I've had to comment out this code before my program even compiles (but try uncommenting it to see the problem):

```
//textBox1.AppendText("b.y=" + b.y + "\r\n");
```

Nor can I get at `y` from inside the `B` class. I've commented out the `Gety()` method of `B`:

```
//public int Gety() {
//    return y;
//}
```

Scope

```
using System;
using System.Windows.Forms;

namespace Scope {

    public class A {
        public int x;
        private int y;
        protected int z;

        public A() {
            x = 100;
            y = 200;
            z = 300;
        }

        public int Gety() {
            return y;
        }

    }

    public class B : A {
        public int Getz() {
            return z;
        }

        //public int Gety() {
        //    return y;
        //}

    }

    public partial class Form1 : Form {
        public Form1() {
            InitializeComponent();
        }

        private void button1_Click(object sender, EventArgs e) {
            B b = new B();
            textBox1.AppendText("b.x=" + b.x + "\r\n");
            // textBox1.AppendText("b.y=" + b.y + "\r\n");
            // textBox1.AppendText("b.z=" + b.z + "\r\n");
            textBox1.AppendText("b.Gety=" + b.Gety() + "\r\n");
            textBox1.AppendText("b.Getz=" + b.Getz() + "\r\n");
        }
    }
}
```

The only place I *can* get at `y` is from within the `A` class where `y` is declared. Here I can write a `Gety()` method to return the value of `y`.

```
public int Gety() {
    return y;
}
```

As this `Gety()` method is `public` I can access it from a `b` object in `Form1`, as I do here:

```
textBox1.AppendText("b.Gety=" + b.Gety() + "\r\n");
```

And finally let's look at `z`. At first sight that seems to be like a `private` variable because I can't call it in the way I can call a `public` variable: `b.z` doesn't work. It's inaccessible. I've had to comment out this line of code too:

```
// textBox1.AppendText("b.z=" + b.z + "\r\n");
```

However, unlike a `private` variable, which, you will remember, is only visible *in the class in which is declared*, a `protected` variable is visible both *in that class, and also in its descendant classes*. So while I can't access `y` from the `B` class because `y` is `private`, I *can* access `z` from the `B` class because `z` is `protected`:

```
public class B : A {
    public int Getz() {
        return z;        // this is ok
    }
}
```

Who needs protected?

Note that while `public` and `private` are widely used access modifiers, `protected` is not so commonly used. In fact, while it may sometimes be useful to define a scope that 'trickles down' through to subclasses, `protected` 'members' (fields and methods) can be confusing. Unless you have a really good reason for defining `protected` members, I would recommend that you stick to using `public` and `private`. It is good practice to make an object's fields (variables) `private` and write `public` methods or properties

Summary

`public` Accessible almost anywhere.

`private` Accessible only within the same class.

`protected` Accessible within the same class, or in a class that descends from it.

Properties

A *property* is a group of one or two special types of method to get (return) or set (assign) the value of a variable. This is a typical definition for a property:

GameClasses

```
private string _name;

public string Name {
    get {
        return _name;
    }
    set {
        _name = value;
    }
}
```

Here `_name` is `private` but `Name` is `public`. This means that code outside the class is able to refer to the `Name` property but not to the `_name` variable. If you omit the `get` part of a property, it will be impossible for code outside the class to retrieve the current value of the associated variable. If you omit the `set` part it will be impossible for code outside the class to assign a new value to the associated variable – in other words, it will be 'read only'.

Alternative Syntax

You can write quite complex code in a property accessor that would let you check a value before setting it, for example, or format a string, do a calculation on a number or perform some other programming task.

An alternative syntax for very simple properties which need to do nothing more than get and set the values of private variables was introduced in version 7 of the C# language. With this alternative syntax you can use an equals sign followed by a right-pointing bracket `=>` both to get a variable and to set it using the keyword `value`. For example, the `Name` property could be written as follows (this is from the *adventure-game* project in Chapter 10):

adventure-game

```
private string _name;

public string Name {
    get => _name;
    set => _name = value;
}
```

Accessing Properties

Even though properties are like pairs of methods, they do not use the same syntax as methods when code refers to them. This is how you might get or set a value using a pair of *methods* named `GetName()` and `SetName()`:

```
myvar = ob.GetName();
ob.SetName("A new name");
```

But the syntax for accessing a *property* is the same as for accessing a public variable. This is how you would get and set a value using a property such as `Name`:

```
myvar = ob.Name;
ob.Name = "A new name";
```

6 – Arrays, Strings and Loops

An array is a list of objects and a string is a list of characters. Processing arrays and strings often requires repetition – we'll see how to do that using loops.

An array is a sequential list. You can think of it as a set of slots in which a fixed number of items can be stored. As with everything else in C#, an array is an object. An array object comes with various methods and properties that can help us to deal with the list of elements stored in the array.

Arrays

A C# array is an instance of the .NET class, `System.Array`. Just like other objects, an array has to be created before it can be used. To see a simple example of this, load up the *Arrays* project and find the `button1_Click()` method. The first line of this method creates and initializes an array of three strings:

Arrays

```
string[] myArray = new string[]{ "one", "two", "three" };
```

The definition of an array begins with the type of the objects it will hold, followed by a pair of square brackets. This array contains strings, so it begins with `string[]`.

Next comes the name of the array, `myArray`. The `new` keyword is responsible for creating the array object. I specify that this array is capable of storing strings so I put `string[]` after `new`.

You can optionally, initialize the array with appropriate objects at the time of its declaration, as I have done here. To initialize the array, I write the array element objects as a comma-delimited list between curly brackets. Here I initialize `myArray` with three strings:

```
{ "one", "two", "three" };
```

Optionally you may place an integer representing the number of array items between square brackets. I have done that in the declaration of `myArray2`:

```
myArray2 = new string[3] { "four", "five", "six" };
```

This integer is not in fact required here because C# can determine the actual number of strings from the items (the three strings) which I have placed between curly brackets. Putting comma-separated array items between curly brackets provides a quick way of initializing an array. Notice that I have even omitted the `new` keyword when declaring and initializing `myArray3`:

```
string[] myArray3 = { "seven", "eight", "nine" };
```

Array Declaration Shortcuts

The 'shortcuts' for defining arrays (omitting the keyword `new` and omitting the number of elements placed between square brackets) are only available when you initialize the array with a fixed number of elements listed between curly brackets. So if you wanted to declare `myArray4` as an array of strings (for example), then, at various points later in your program, add some strings one at a time, you would have to declare the array variable like this:

```
string[] myArray4 = new string[3];
```

The shorthand way of creating and initializing an array without using the `new` keyword is only available when you do this in a single line of code. If you declare the array variable first and initialize it later, you must create the array object using `new`, like this:

```
string[] myArray2;                                  // declare
myArray2 = new string[3]{ "four", "five", "six" };   // initialize
```

An array can, in principle, hold any type of object. The `myObjectArray` array, for example, holds three objects of the class, `MyClass`:

```
MyClass[] myObjectArray = new MyClass[3];
```

Loops

To iterate over the items in an array, you may want to write some sort of loop. A loop may contain some code that is run repeatedly. In the *Arrays* project you will see several `for` loops. The first `for` loop, fills `MyObjectArray` with three objects of the `MyClass` type:

Arrays

```
for(int i = 0; i <= 2; i++) {
    myObjectArray[i] = new MyClass("Object #" + i + ". ");
}
```

Arrays in C# are *0-based*, which means that the first item of a three-element array is at index 0 and the last item is at index 2. A position in an array is indicated by the index number between square brackets.

for Loops

Here is another simple example of a `for` loop:

```
for (int i = 1; i < 100; i++) {
     dosomething();
}
```

The code between the parentheses after the word `for` is used to control the execution of the loop. This code is divided into three parts:

1. `int i = 1` The first part initializes an `int` variable, `i`, with the value 1.

2. `i < 100` The second part contains a test. The loop executes as long as this test remains true. Here the test states that the value of the variable `i` must be less than 100.

3. `i++` Finally, I have to be sure to increment the value of `i` at each turn through the loop. That happens in the third part of the loop control statement which adds 1 to the value of `i`.

So, this loop control statement -

```
for (int i = 1; i < 100; i++)
```

- could be expressed, in English, as:

Let i equal 1.
While i is less than 100 execute the code inside the loop.
Then add 1 to i.

Note that this loop will execute 99 times, not 100, since it will fail when the value of `i` is no longer *less than* 100. Now look at loop 2 in the sample code:

```
for(int i = 0; i <= myArray.Length - 1; i++) {
    textBox1.Text = textBox1.Text + myArray[i] + ". ";
}
```

This loop iterates through the list of strings in `myArray` and displays them in `textBox1`. Note the expression in second part of the `for` loop:

```
i <= myArray.Length - 1
```

Instead of using a fixed number, such as 2, to specify final index of the array, I've used the array object's `Length` property. However, since `Length` is always 1 greater than the index (remember that arrays are indexed from 0, so the first item is at index 0, the second at index 1 and so on), I have subtracted 1 from `Length`.

In loop 3 I have used two of the methods that .NET provides specifically for use with arrays, `GetLowerBound(0)` and `GetUpperBound(0)`, to determine the start and end indices of `myArray2`:

```
for(int i = myArray2.GetLowerBound(0); i <= myArray2.GetUpperBound(0); i++) {
    textBox2.Text = textBox2.Text + myArray2[i] + ". ";
}
```

These methods return the actual indices (here 0 and 2) of the array's first and last elements. Using these two methods makes the code more generic since it will work with arrays of any size. The 0 argument here indicates that I am testing the first *dimension* of an array. In fact, this array only has one dimension. C# can work with multi-dimensional arrays (arrays containing other arrays) too.

The code of loop 4 shows how similar techniques can be used to iterate through an array of user-defined objects and retrieve values (here the `Name` property) from each in turn:

```
for(int i = 0; i <= myObjectArray.GetUpperBound(0); i++) {
    textBox3.Text = textBox3.Text + myObjectArray[i].Name;
}
```

foreach Loops

The next loop in the *Arrays* project (loop 5) is a bit more interesting. Instead of using `for` it uses `foreach`. The `foreach` statement iterates through each element in an array without any need for an indexing variable.

A `foreach` loop is controlled by specifying the data type (here `MyClass`), an identifier to be used within the loop (here `myob`), and the name of the array or the collection (here `myObjectArray`):

Arrays

```
foreach(MyClass myob in myObjectArray) {
    textBox4.Text = textBox4.Text + myob.Name;
}
```

At each turn through the loop, the next `MyClass` object in `myObjectArray` is assigned to the variable, `myob`. I can then access this object's methods or properties, such as `Name`.

while Loops

Sometimes you may want to execute some code an uncertain number of times – that is, while some test condition remains `true`. To do that, use a `while` loop. The *WordCount* project (shown on the next page) uses several `while` loops.

These `while` loops may test a single condition as in this loop in the `CountWordsAndCharacters()` method which runs the code as long as the value of `charcount` is less than the length of the string `s`:

```
while(charcount < s.Length){
    // code to be run
}
```

WordCount

```
char[] DELIMS = new char[10] {' ', '.', ',', '?', '!', '-', '_', '+', '*', '/'};
int charcount = 0;

private bool IsDelimiter(char c) {
    bool delimfound = false;
    foreach (char mychar in DELIMS) {
        if (mychar == c)
            delimfound = true;
    }
    return delimfound;
}

private void FindDelims() {
    string s = richTextBox1.Text;
    int delimcount = 0;
    for (int i = 0; i < s.Length; i++) {
        if (IsDelimiter(s[i]))
            delimcount++;
    }
    MessageBox.Show("delimcount=" + delimcount,"Statistics",MessageBoxButtons.OK,
        MessageBoxIcon.Information);
}

private bool ScrollThroughWord(string s) {
    bool wordfound = false;
    while ((charcount < s.Length) && !(IsDelimiter(s[charcount]))) {
        charcount++;
        wordfound = true;
    }
    return wordfound;
}

private void ScrollThroughDelims(string s) {
    while ((charcount < s.Length) && IsDelimiter(s[charcount])) {
        charcount++;
    }
}

private void CountWordsAndCharacters() {
    string s = textBox1.Text;
    charcount = 0;
    int wordcount = 0;
    while (charcount < s.Length) {
        ScrollThroughDelims(s);
        if (ScrollThroughWord(s)) {
            wordcount++;
        }
    }
    this.Text = "Number of words: " + wordcount + " Characters: " + charcount;
}
```

WordCount (continued)

```
private void button1_Click(object sender, System.EventArgs e) {
    FindDelims();
}

private void button3_Click(object sender, EventArgs e) {
    CountWordsAndCharacters();
}
```

A `while` loop may also test multiple conditions, as here in the `ScrollThroughDelims()` method:

```
while((charcount < s.Length) && IsDelimiter(s[charcount]))
```

This runs the code in the loop only as long as *both* of *two* conditions remain true:

1. The value of `charcount` is less than the length of `s`
   and (&&)
2. The Boolean value returned from the `IsDelimiter()` method when passed the character at the `charcount` index of the string `s` is *true*.

Boolean

As explained in Chapter 2, a Boolean value is one that is either `true` or `false`. The C# `bool` data type is used to represent Boolean values. My `IsDelimiter()` method returns a `bool`:

```
private bool IsDelimiter(char c)
```

Here is another example. You will find this code in the `ScrollThroughWord()` method. This looks almost the same as the last `while` loop. In fact, the exclamation mark `!` changes everything. This time, in order for the entire test to evaluated to `true`, the Boolean value returned from the `IsDelimiter()` method must return `false`. That is because `!` is the *not* operator:

```
!(IsDelimiter(s[charcount]))
```

The `!` operator negates this test. That means the test `IsDelimiter(s[charcount])` only succeeds if it is *not true*; in other words, if it is *false*.

do...while Loops

In some circumstances, you may want to be certain that the code within a loop runs at least once. For example, you might want to prompt the user to enter some data – and you need to ensure that this is done *at least once*.

One way of doing that would be to write a `do...while` loop. A `do...while` loop is essentially the same as a `while` loop, apart from the fact that the test condition is placed at the *end* of the loop rather than at the beginning. This means that the statements inside the loop are bound to execute *at least once* before the test condition is even evaluated. This is the syntax of a `do...while` loop:

```
do {
   // one or more statements
} while (condition);
```

Here is a very simple example of a `do...while` loop:

DoWhile

```
int[] intarray = { 1, 2, 3, 4, 5 };
int i;
i = 2;

do {
    Console.WriteLine(intarray[i]);
    i++;
} while (i < 2);
```

Here the test condition, `(i < 2)`, evaluates to `false` the first time it is tested. But since this test is only performed *after* the code in the loop, that code is run *once*. In this case, this output is shown (the integer at index 2 in `intarray`):

```
3
```

Compare that with this `while` loop:

```
i = 2;
while (i < 2) {
    Console.WriteLine(intarray[i]);
    i++;
}
```

Here the test, `(i < 2)`, is the same as the test that I used in the `do...while` loop. However, this time the test is evaluated at the *start* of the loop. It evaluates to `false` so the code inside the loop *never* executes. Not even once.

That is an important difference to understand between a regular `while` loop with the test condition at the *start* and a `do...while` loop that has the test at the *end* of the code to be run. No matter what happens, a `do...while` loop will run at least once. But in some cases, if the test condition evaluate to `false` right away, then the code inside a regular `while` loop may never run at all.

Up to know we've looked at arrays that contain strings, integers or other types of object and we've seen how to use loops to iterate through the elements in an array. A string is, in some ways, quite a similar structure to an array. It contains a sequential list of characters. And, like an array, a string can be indexed to find characters at a specific position. We will now look at strings and characters in more detail.

string and char

In C#, a string can be entered as a series of characters delimited by double quotes like this: `"Hello world"`. The data type is `string` (in lower case). This is a shorthand alias for `System.String` in the .NET framework.

String objects can make use of a broad range of methods belonging to the `System.String` class. There are methods to find substrings, to trim blank spaces and to return a copy of a string in upper or lower case. To find the length of a string, you can use the `Length` property.

char

A single character has the `char` data type and is delimited by single quotes:

```
char mychar = 'a';
```

The characters in a string can be accessed by specifying an integer to index into the string. Just like arrays, strings are zero-based so the first character is at position 0 rather than 1.

Assume that the string `s` contains the text, `"Hello world!"`. The expression, `s.Length`, would return a value of 12. This returns the number of characters in the string from `'H'` to `'!'`.

However, in order to assign the first character, `'H'`, and the 12th character, `'!'`, to the char variables, `c1` and `c2`, you would need to index into the string at position 0 (the first character) and position 11 (the length of the string minus 1):

```
char c1 = s[0];
char c2 = s[11];
```

To see some working examples, try out the code in the *Strings* project. This code shows the length of a string:

```
Strings
textBox2.Text = "Length: " + textBox1.Text.Length;
```

Assuming that the `Text` (a `string`) of `textBox1` is `"Hello world!"` (which contains twelve characters including a space and '!'), this is what will be shown in `textBox2`:

```
Length: 12
```

This next bit of code iterates over the characters in the string of `textBox1.Text` and then displays each character and its index:

```
string s = textBox1.Text;
string s2 = "";
for (int i = 0; i < s.Length; i++) {
    s2 += "[" + i + "]='" + s[i] + "' ";
}
textBox2.Text = s2;
```

The `Text` of `textBox2` shows this:

```
[0]='H' [1]='e' [2]='l' [3]='l' [4]='o' [5]=' ' [6]='w' [7]='o' [8]='r' [9]='l'
[10]='d' [11]='!'
```

String Operations

Strings in C# can be manipulated in numerous ways using built-in methods. Here I just want to show a few examples of some common methods. You may want refer to Microsoft's online documentation for a full list of string methods.

It is normal to create strings by assigning literal strings, between double-quote characters, to the `string` type like this:

```
string s = "Hello";
```

In the code above, you are creating a `string` object called `s` and that object has access to the methods of the `String` class (the lowercase `string` data type is actually an 'alias' for the `System.String` class).

Concatenation is probably the most common string operation: adding one string onto the end of another one. While the `String` class has a `Concat()` method that can do this, it is more usual to use the `+` operator. We've already used that many times in the sample programs in this book:

```
s = s + " world";
```

Or you can combine concatenation and assignment by using the `+=` operator like this:

```
s += " world\r\n";
```

Escape Characters

Sometimes you may want to embed non-printing characters into strings. These can be entered as character codes after a \ character. The most common (which we've already used many times) is the newline character `'\n'`. Other common escape characters include carriage return `'\r'` and tab `'\t'`. Note that some .NET controls (such as the `TextBox` used here) require a carriage return followed by a newline character (`"\r\n"`) in order to move the focus to a new line in the control. If you want to enter a double-quote character in a double-quoted string, do this: `"\""` You can enter a backslash character like this: `"\\"`. This is an example from the *EscapeChars* sample project:

EscapeChars

```
string s = "Hello world\nTab\t, \\ and \" ";
textBox1.Text = s;
```

This output is shown in `textBox1`:

```
Helloworld
Tab     , a \ and a "
```

The *StringOps* sample project shows examples of various string methods. I've numbered each example so you can easily compare the output with the code:

StringOps

```
static void Main(string[] args) {
    string s = "Hello";
    s += " World";
    Char[] TrimChars = { ' ', '*', '-' };
    StringBuilder sb = new StringBuilder("Hello World");
    Console.WriteLine("1  " + s.ToUpper());
    Console.WriteLine("2  " + s.ToLower());
    Console.WriteLine("3  " + s.PadLeft(30));
    Console.WriteLine("4  " + s.PadLeft(30, '-'));
    Console.WriteLine("5  " + s.PadRight(30, '*'));
    Console.WriteLine("6  " + s.IndexOf("World"));
    Console.WriteLine("7  " + s.IndexOf("Moon"));
    Console.WriteLine("8  " + s.Replace("World", "Moon"));
    Console.WriteLine("9  " + s);
    // --- StringBuilder
    Console.WriteLine("10 " + sb.Replace("World", "Moon"));
    Console.WriteLine("11 " + sb);
    sb.Append(" - and goodbye");
    Console.WriteLine("12 " + sb);
    s = "         " + s + "-*-*-";
    Console.WriteLine("13 " + s);
    Console.WriteLine("14 " + s.TrimStart());
    Console.WriteLine("15  " + s.TrimEnd(TrimChars));
    Console.WriteLine("16  " + s.Trim(TrimChars));
}
```

This is the output:

```
1  HELLO WORLD
2  hello world
3                    Hello World
4  -------------------Hello World
5  Hello World*******************
6  6
7  -1
8  Hello Moon
9  Hello World
10 Hello Moon
11 Hello Moon
12 Hello Moon - and goodbye
13          Hello World-*-*-
14 Hello World-*-*-
15          Hello World
16  Hello World
```

1. `ToUpper()` returns an uppercase version of the string stored in `s`.
2. `ToLower()` returns a lowercase version of the string stored in `s`.
3. `PadLeft()` adds spaces (padding characters) to the left of the string to pad out the entire string to the length specified.
4. `PadLeft()` can also pad a string using a specific character instead of a space (here '-') as a second argument.
5. `PadRight()` has the same options as `PadLeft()` but it adds characters to the right of the string.
6. `IndexOf()` returns the index of a substring. Here `"World"` is found at index 6 in `s`.
7. If the substring is not found by `IndexOf()` as here – with the substring `"Moon"` – then -1 is returned.
8. `Replace()` replaces one string with another.
9. and 13. `+` concatenates two strings.

14. `TrimStart()` trims chars from the start of a string.
15. `TrimEnd()` trims chars from the end of a string.
16. `Trim()` trims chars from both the start and the end of a string.

The three trimming methods return a trimmed string. By default 'whitespace' chars (non-printing characters such as spaces and tabs) are trimmed. If you want to remove other specific characters you can define an array of the characters to be removed and pass that as an argument to `TrimStart()`, `TrimEnd()` or `Trim()`:

```
Char[] TrimChars = { ' ', '*', '-' };

Console.WriteLine("15   " + s.TrimEnd(TrimChars));
Console.WriteLine("16   " + s.Trim(TrimChars));
```

But what about operations 10, 11 and 12? These are not applied the `string s` but to a `StringBuilder` variable, `sb`. So what is the difference between `string` and `StringBuilder`? I'll explain that next.

StringBuilder

The main difference between a `StringBuilder` object and a `string` is that a `StringBuilder` object can be changed whereas a `string` can't. At first sight, it may seem that we made changes to strings when we used methods such as `ToUpper()`, `ToLower()`, `Replace()` and so on? But, in fact, we didn't.

Each of those `String` methods creates a *new* string which is set to uppercase or lowercase or which has one substring replaced by another. The *original* `string` object (here that's the variable `s`), remains unchanged.

A new `StringBuilder` object can be created and initialized with a `string` as an argument:

```
StringBuilder sb = new StringBuilder("Hello World");
```

To understand how it differs from a `string`, look at this example. Here I call `Replace()` with the `string` object s, to replace the substring `"World"` with `"Moon"`:

```
Console.WriteLine("8  " + s.Replace("World", "Moon"));
Console.WriteLine("9  " + s);
```

This yields a new string object. The original string `s`, remains unchanged. I can verify this by displaying first the value yielded by `Replace()`:

```
8  Hello Moon
```

And then, I display the `string`, `s`, which remains unchanged:

```
9  Hello World
```

If I wanted to change the value of `s` itself I would need to make an assignment:

```
s = s.Replace("World", "Moon");
```

That would assign the new string object (the value yielded by `Replace()`) to the variable `s`. But when I do the same operation on a `StringBuilder` object `sb` (that is, I replace `"World"` with `"Moon"`), I make no assignment back to `sb`:

```
Console.WriteLine("10 " + sb.Replace("World", "Moon"));
Console.WriteLine("11 " + sb);
sb.Append(" - and goodbye");
Console.WriteLine("12 " + sb);
```

And yet the value of `sb` itself has been changed. If I now call `Append()` to append another string, again `sb` is changed:

```
10 Hello Moon
11 Hello Moon
12 Hello Moon - and goodbye
```

So, in brief, strings are *immutable* – they cannot be changed. You can only create *new* `string` objects and then, if you wish, you can assign those new objects to a variable (which might be original `string` variable). But a `StringBuilder` object is *mutable* – it can be changed.

Why does that matter? For now, while you are learning C#, it probably doesn't matter very much. Most of the time, strings will do everything you need. `StringBuilder` objects only really come into their own when a program makes *lots* of changes to strings *repeatedly*. It is more efficient to make changes to a `StringBuilder` object by, for example, adding characters onto the end of an *existing* `string`, instead of using a regular `string` object to return *new* strings. There may come a time when this sort of efficiency matters to you, but for now it's likely to be simpler and easier to stick to normal strings.

Incidentally, you can convert a `StringBuilder` object to a regular string using the `ToString()` method:

```
s = sb.ToString();
```

Format Strings

I first mentioned the very useful `String.Format()` method back in Chapter 2. You may recall that the `Format()` method provides a simple way of substituting values from variables or expressions into a string.

The string is passed to the method as the first argument, and a comma-delimited list of values is placed after the string. Numbered placeholders between curly brackets are placed into the string. Values from the comma-delimited list will be inserted or 'interpolated' at the positions of the placeholders:

StringInterpolation

```
string s = "";
string mystring = "Test";

s = String.Format("{0}. {1}. {2}. {3}", mystring, 1 + 2, "hello world".ToUpper(),
Multiply(10, 5));
Console.WriteLine(s);
```

The above code displays this:

```
Test. 3. HELLO WORLD. 50
```

The first value, which is at index 0 (here that's the variable `mystring`) replaces the `{0}` placeholder, the second value at index 1 (here that's `3` – the value returned from the expression `1+2`) replaces the `{1}` placeholder and so on.

You can see from this example, that I am not limited to displaying a simple variable. I can also show the result of a calculation, I can call a method on an object such as `"hello world".ToUpper()`. I can even call a function of my own such as `Multiply(10, 5)` and display its return value:

```
public static int Multiply(int x, int y) {
    return x * y;
}
```

You don't have to display the arguments in the order in which they appear in the list. In the next example, I display them in reverse order, the 5th argument, that's the value 6, then the 4th which has the value 5 and so on down to the first value at index 0 which is 1, and I also repeat the arguments `{5}`, `{4}` and `{3}`:

```
s = String.Format("{5} {4} {3} {2} {1} {0} {5} {4} {3} ", 1, 2, 3, 4, 5, 6);
Console.WriteLine(s);
```

This displays:

```
6 5 4 3 2 1 6 5 4
```

String interpolation

As an alternative to using `String.Format()` with numbered placeholders, C# also lets you include expressions right inside the string itself. This is called string interpolation. This feature was first introduced in version 6 of the C# language.

To create an interpolated string you need to precede the string itself with the `$` character. You should place any expressions that you want to be evaluated between pairs of curly brackets in the string. This is an example:

StringInterpolation

```
s = $"(a) {mystring} of string interpolation: 1+2 = {1 + 2}. {"hello ↵
world".ToUpper()}. {Multiply(10, 5)}";
Console.WriteLine(s);
```

Assuming that the `mystring` variable has been assigned the string `"Test"`, this is the output:

```
(a) Test of string interpolation: 1+2 = 3. HELLO WORLD. 50
```

It turns out that the `WriteLine()` method of `Console`, which is used to display a string in a command window, will evaluate these expressions even without preceding the string with a `$` symbol. But this is a 'special case'. Usually, the dollar symbol is needed when you want to evaluate expressions embedded into strings in this way.

Remember that even ordinary strings (without the preceding `$`) evaluate certain special characters (see the note on 'Escape Characters' earlier in this chapter). For example, they will substitute a newline for `\n` and a tab for `\t` as shown here.

```
s = "\nThis is a \t{mystring}\n";        // regular string
Console.WriteLine(s);
```

This displays:

```
This is a       {mystring}
!!
```

Special characters such as newlines and tabs are also evaluated in interpolated strings:

```
s = $"\nThis is a \t{mystring}\n!!";     // interpolated
Console.WriteLine(s);
```

This displays:

```
This is a       Test
!!
```

Verbatim Strings

But what if you want to prevent any evaluation (that is, you want the string to be displayed *exactly* as you wrote it, with no code evaluation and no substitution of characters such as `\t` and `\n`)? In that case, you need to create a verbatim string.

To create a verbatim string, you must put a `@` symbol in front of the string, as in this example:

```
s = @"\r\nThis is a \t{mystring}\n!!";        // verbatim
Console.WriteLine(s);
```

When this code displays the string, nothing is evaluated – even `\r`, `\n` and `\t` are shown literally:

```
\r\nThis is a \t{mystring}\n!!
```

Dialogs and Message Boxes

This chapters' projects use several different types of dialog box. You may have noticed that the *WordCount* project uses the `MessageBox` dialog. This is defined entirely in code:

WordCount

```
MessageBox.Show("delimcount=" + delimcount,
    "Statistics",
    MessageBoxButtons.OK,
    MessageBoxIcon.Information);
```

Here the `MessageBox.Show()` method is passed a number of arguments to display a string, one or more buttons and an icon. Refer to the .NET help system for a full explanation.

C# Help in Visual Studio

If you are looking for help on a .NET method or class, highlight the name (e.g. `MessageBox`) in the Visual Studio code editor and press **F1**. This will load online help into your web browser.

Sample Program: Editor

The *Editor* project implements a simple text editor that can load and save text and rich text (RTF) format files. You could use this project to experiment with string methods. For example, you could try adding features to format text in upper or lower case. I've added a *Tools* menu with a *Word count* option. At present, word counting is not implemented. However, if you look back at my *WordCount* project you'll find guidance on how to program that. You might want to play around with this project and see if you can add a word counter to the *Editor*.

The *Editor* project uses *OpenFile* and *SaveFile* dialogs which are displayed when menu items are clicked in the application's *File* menu:

Editor

```
private void menuItem2_Click(object sender, EventArgs e) {
    openFile1.DefaultExt = "rtf";
    openFile1.Filter = "RTF Files (*.rtf)|*.rtf|Text files (*.txt)|*.txt";

    if (openFile1.ShowDialog() == DialogResult.OK &&
        openFile1.FileName.Length > 0) { // Load file into the RichTextBox
        if (openFile1.FilterIndex == 1) {
            richTextBox1.LoadFile(openFile1.FileName,
                RichTextBoxStreamType.RichText)
        } else
            richTextBox1.LoadFile(openFile1.FileName,
                RichTextBoxStreamType.PlainText
    }

}

private void menuItem6_Click(object sender, EventArgs e) {
    saveFile1.DefaultExt = "rtf";
    saveFile1.Filter = "RTF Files (*.rtf)|*.rtf|Text files (*.txt)|*.txt";

    if (saveFile1.ShowDialog() == DialogResult.OK &&
        saveFile1.FileName.Length > 0) {
        saveFile1.AddExtension = true;
        if (System.IO.Path.GetExtension(saveFile1.FileName) == "") {
            saveFile1.FileName = saveFile1.FileName + ".xxx";
        }
        // Save contents of RichTextBox to file.
        if (saveFile1.FilterIndex == 1) {
            richTextBox1.SaveFile(saveFile1.FileName,
                 RichTextBoxStreamType.RichText)
        } else
            richTextBox1.SaveFile(saveFile1.FileName,
             RichTextBoxStreamType.PlainText
    }
}
```

These dialogs are configured by setting properties in code – such as the default file extension, *DefaultExt*, and the *Filter* (these are the file extensions that will be available from the dialog's File Type selector).

You can, if you wish, create *Open* and *Save* dialogs in code, like this:

```
OpenFileDialog openFile1 = new OpenFileDialog();
```

However, in this project, I simply dropped the two File dialog controls from the Visual Studio Toolbox into the Designer. This has the benefit that their properties can be set using the Properties panel. In fact, if you wish, you can delete the *Filter* and *DefaultExt* assignments from the code and use the Properties panel to set them instead.

7 – Files and Directories

File-handling is one of the essential skills of programming. In this chapter we look at how to write programs that use files and IO (Input/Output) in C#.

Whether you are programming a spreadsheet, a web browser, a word processor or a game, you will, at some stage, have to read data from one place and write it to another. In this chapter I shall explore the classes and techniques that you will need to master all kinds of data reading and writing operations in C#.

Files and IO

The *Editor* project from the last chapter implemented a simple text editor which is able to load and save text files to be displayed in a `RichTextBox` control. The `RichTextBox` control has its own `SaveFile()` and `LoadFile()` methods.

So, for example, if the main form of the user interface includes a `RichTextBox` control named `textBox1`, this is how you would save its contents to a file whose name the user had entered into a `SaveFileDialog` component named `saveFile1` (that is, as the `FileName` property):

```
textBox1.SaveFile(saveFile1.FileName, RichTextBoxStreamType.RichText);
```

The final parameter in the code above, `RichTextBoxStreamType.RichText`, specifies that rich text formatting, including font styles, is to be retained. To save it as simple ASCII text (text that does not retain colours, font styles and so on), you would need to replace `RichText` with `PlainText`:

```
textBox1.SaveFile(saveFile1.FileName, RichTextBoxStreamType.PlainText);
```

Saving data is extremely easy if you happen to be saving it from a `RichTextBox` control, which has this behaviour 'built in'. But what if you happen to be saving data from your own, non-visual objects or loading data from a file that contains non-text data?

Before I explain the programming techniques you will require in order to save data to disk, we first need to learn a bit about the IO (Input/Output) features of the .NET framework. In particular, I want to explain the concept of a 'stream'.

Streams

A stream is a sequence of bytes (a byte is a chunk of data approximately corresponding to a single character) that can flow from one place to another. Often it will flow from the hard disk into memory or vice versa. But a stream could equally flow from one place in memory to another place in memory or from one computer to another.

Variations on a Stream

There are various 'specialised' types of stream in .NET but here I want to concentrate on the essential features of streams in general. Let's start by seeing how to use basic `Stream` objects to make a copy of a file. In this project, we will be making copies of the file, *Text.txt*. My code assumes that this file can be found in the *Test* directory on the C drive.

If you want to try out my sample project, first use the Windows Explorer to create the *Test* directory on your C drive and copy the *Test.txt* file (from *Step07**streams*) into it. If you fail to do this, the sample program will not work! Be sure to keep the Windows Explorer open on the *C:**Test* directory when you run the program so you can see which files are created.

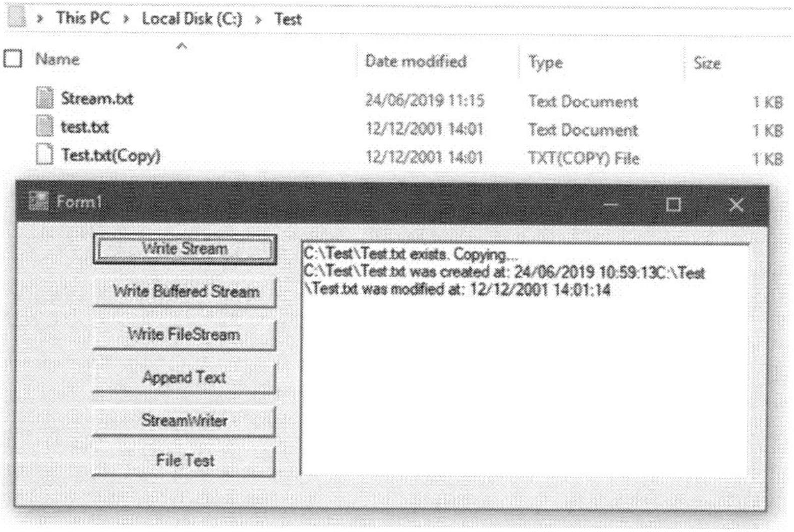

Now load up the *Streams* project. Scroll to the top of the code editor. You will see that I have specified the source file and directory here:

```
Streams
const string SOURCEFN = "C:\\Test\\test.txt";
```

Note that I have also added `System.IO` to the `using` section at the top of the code. The `System.IO` namespace contains all the essential IO classes that we'll need such as `File`, `StreamWriter`, `StreamReader` and the entire hierarchy of Streams.

Missing namespace?

If you forget to add `System.IO` to the `using` section of your code, Visual Studio will show errors. Right-click the missing class name (e.g. `Stream`) in the editor and select '*Quick Actions and Refactorings*'. Then select `using System.IO;` to add this automatically.

Switch to the Form Designer. You can switch between the Code View and the Design view using the *View* menu of Visual Studio or the default hotkeys (`SHIFT-F7` for the Designer, `F7` for Code). Double-click the top button, labelled '*Write Stream*'. This will take you to the button's event-handling method: `WriteStreamBtn_Click()`:

```
Streams
private void WriteStreamBtn_Click( object sender, System.EventArgs e ) {
    const string OUTPUTFN = "C:\\Test\\Stream.txt";
    Stream instream = File.OpenRead(SOURCEFN);
    Stream outstream = File.OpenWrite(OUTPUTFN);
    byte[] buffer = new Byte[BUFFSIZE];
    int numbytes;

    while((numbytes = instream.Read( buffer, 0, BUFFSIZE )) > 0) {
        outstream.Write(buffer, 0, numbytes);
    }
    instream.Close();
    outstream.Close();
}
```

The method begins with the declaration of the output file name, `OUTPUTFN`, and I then create two stream objects:

```
const string OUTPUTFN = "C:\\Test\\Stream.txt";
Stream instream = File.OpenRead(SOURCEFN);
Stream outstream = File.OpenWrite(OUTPUTFN);
```

Notice that I use double-slashes `"\\"` to separate the directory names in the string. That's because a single slash in a string is used to indicate that the letter following it represents a special character. For example `"\n"` is a new line and `"\t"` is a tab. When I want to put an actual `'\'` character in a string, I need to precede it by another `'\'` character which is what I've done here: `"C:\\Test\\Stream.txt"`

Each stream is created by methods of the `File` class. The `OpenRead()` and `OpenWrite()` methods create files for reading and writing and they each return a `FileStream` object.

static Methods

`OpenRead()` and `OpenWrite()` are `static` methods of the `File` class. This means that you can use them by referring to the `File` class itself rather than to a specific `File` object. You can think of a `static` method as a method that 'belongs' to the class rather than to an individual object created from the class. I'll have more to say on `static` methods in Chapter 8.

Now I create a 'buffer' (an area of memory used for temporary storage) into which to read data. This buffer is an array of 1024 bytes (I set the `BUFFSIZE` constant to 1024 at the top of the code):

```
byte[] buffer = new Byte[BUFFSIZE];
```

A `while` loop continually reads bytes from the input stream, `instream`, into this buffer as long as there are more bytes to be read (the reading is all done inside the parentheses at the start of this `while` loop and the bytes read are assigned to the `numbytes` variable until the value is 0 when there are no more bytes to be read). The bytes (whose total number is stored in `numbytes`) are then written into the output stream, `outstream`:

```
while((numbytes = instream.Read(buffer, 0, BUFFSIZE)) > 0) {
    outstream.Write(buffer, 0, numbytes);
}
```

When all the reading and writing is completed, the two streams are closed:

```
instream.Close();
outstream.Close();
```

The real problem with this code is that it is inefficient since it reads and writes data one byte at a time. You may not notice this when working with a small file. But it might be noticeable when working with very long files.

I could make the code more efficient by reading larger 'blocks' of bytes all in one go. I can do this by creating a `BufferedStream` object. You can see an example of this in the `BuffStreamWriteBtn_Click()` method:

Streams

```
private void BuffStreamWriteBtn_Click(object sender, System.EventArgs e) {
    const string OUTPUTFN = "C:\\Test\\BuffStream.txt";
    Stream instream = File.OpenRead(SOURCEFN);
    Stream outstream = File.OpenWrite(OUTPUTFN);
    BufferedStream buffInput = new BufferedStream(instream);
    BufferedStream buffOutput = new BufferedStream(outstream);
    byte[] buffer = new Byte[BUFFSIZE];
    int numbytes;

    while ((numbytes = buffInput.Read(buffer, 0, BUFFSIZE)) > 0) {
        buffOutput.Write(buffer, 0, numbytes);
    }
    buffInput.Close();
    buffOutput.Close();
}
```

The only significant difference from the previous method we looked at is that that this one uses buffered stream objects rather than basic stream objects. To ensure that all data is written ('flushed') to disk, the `BufferedStream` class provides the `Flush()` method. However, when the output stream is closed by the `Close()` method, any buffered data is automatically flushed, so it is not necessary to call the `Flush()` method here.

The `FileStreamBtn_Click()` method implements an equivalent file-copying routine to the one we've just looked at. It combines the efficiency of a `BufferedStream` with the simplicity of an unbuffered `Stream`:

```
Streams
private void FileStreamBtn_Click(object sender, System.EventArgs e) {
     const string OUTPUTFN = "C:\\Test\\FileStream.txt";
     FileStream instream = new FileStream(SOURCEFN, FileMode.OpenOrCreate,
                                           FileAccess.Read);
     FileStream outstream = new FileStream(OUTPUTFN, FileMode.OpenOrCreate,
                                           FileAccess.Write)
     byte[] buffer = new Byte[BUFFSIZE];
     int bytesRead;

     while ((bytesRead = instream.Read(buffer, 0, BUFFSIZE)) > 0) {
         outstream.Write(buffer, 0, bytesRead);
     }
     instream.Close();
     outstream.Close();
 }
```

There is much more to `FileStream` than I have space to explore here because it comes with many methods that can assist in file handling. Refer to the online .NET help documentation for information. The only new feature here is the `FileStream` constructor:

```
FileStream instream = new FileStream(SOURCEFN,              //name
                                     FileMode.OpenOrCreate, //mode
                                     FileAccess.Read);      //access
```

The `FileStream` class has several constructors. The one I use here takes the three arguments: the *file name* parameter, the *file mode* parameter (which is a pre-declared constant that specifies how to open or create a file) and the *file access* parameter which is a constant that determines whether the file can be read from or written to.

The three file copying methods I've created up to now, operate on bytes and can be used to copy data of any type. I've used them to copy text files but they could just as well be used to copy an executable file or some other sort of binary data. If the input file were *wordpad.exe* and the output file were named *mycopy.exe*, all three of my file-copying routines would make a correct copy of the *wordpad.exe* program.

Reading and Writing Text Files

There is another way of handling files containing plain text:

```
Streams
private void StreamWriterBtn_Click(object sender, System.EventArgs e) {
    const string OUTPUTFN = "C:\\Test\\StreamWriter.txt";
    StreamReader sread;
    StreamWriter swrite;
    String aline;

    if (!File.Exists(SOURCEFN)) {
        MessageBox.Show(SOURCEFN + " does not exist!", "File not found.",
            MessageBoxButtons.OK, MessageBoxIcon.Exclamation);
    } else {
        sread = File.OpenText(SOURCEFN);
        swrite = File.CreateText(OUTPUTFN);
        while ((aline = sread.ReadLine()) != null) {
            swrite.WriteLine(aline);
        }
        sread.Close();
        swrite.Close();
    }
}
```

My `StreamWriterBtn_Click()` method, uses the `StreamReader` and `StreamWriter` classes to read and write a text file one line at a time. A line is defined as a sequence of characters followed by a line feed (`"\n"`) or a carriage return immediately followed by a line feed (`"\r\n"`). The string that is returned by the `ReadLine()` method of `StreamReader` does not contain the terminating carriage return or line feed. Unlike the classes I've used previously, the `StreamReader` and `StreamWriter` classes are not descendants of the `Stream` class. Instead, they operate *upon* Stream objects.

The `File` class provides the methods, `OpenText()` and `CreateText()`. When a file name is passed as an argument, these methods return a `StreamReader` or a `StreamWriter` object:

```
sread = File.OpenText(SOURCEFN);
swrite = File.CreateText(OUTPUTFN);
```

To read a line, use `StreamReader`'s `ReadLine()` method. To write a line use, `StreamWriter`'s `WriteLine() method`. In my code, a `while` loop reads through the lines of text from the input file. The lines of text are read in by the `StreamReader` object, `sread`, as long as there are more lines to be read - that is, until `null` is returned (`null` is a value that indicates that an object is not referenced by a variable, as explained in Chapter 5). The string variable, `aline`, is initialized with the current line which is then written by the `StreamWriter` object, `swrite`, to the output file:

```
while ((aline = sread.ReadLine()) != null) {
    swrite.WriteLine(aline);
}
```

In a finished application, it would be good practice always to test whether a file exists before attempting to read data from it. The `StreamWriterBtn_Click()` method does this using this test:

```
if(!File.Exists(SOURCEFN))
```

Appending Data To A File

There may be occasions when you want to modify an existing file. For instance, if you are working with plain text files (or other file types such as RTF, which contain ordinary ASCII 'text' characters), you might want to add some text to the end of the file. The `AppendBtn_Click()` method in the *Streams* project does that:

Streams

```
private void AppendBtn_Click(object sender, System.EventArgs e) {
    const string OUTPUTFN = "C:\\Test\\FileStream.txt";
    StreamReader sread;
    StreamWriter swrite;
    String aline;
    if (!File.Exists(SOURCEFN)) {
        MessageBox.Show(SOURCEFN + " does not exist!",
            "File not found.",
            MessageBoxButtons.OK,
            MessageBoxIcon.Exclamation);
    } else if (!File.Exists(OUTPUTFN)) {
        MessageBox.Show(OUTPUTFN + " does not exist!",
            "File not found.",
            MessageBoxButtons.OK,
            MessageBoxIcon.Exclamation);
```

Streams (continued)

```
    } else {
        sread = File.OpenText(SOURCEFN);
        swrite = File.AppendText(OUTPUTFN);
        while ((aline = sread.ReadLine()) != null) {
            swrite.WriteLine(aline);
        }
        sread.Close();
        swrite.Close();
    }
}
```

The `StreamWriter` object, `swrite`, uses the `File` class's `AppendText()` method to write text at the end of any text that is already in the specified file. If the specified file does not exist, then it is created ready for text to be written into it.

The File Class

If you are dealing with files in .NET, it is worth getting to know the `File` class. All the methods of this class are `static` so you won't have to create new `File` objects in order to use them. In the example code shown earlier I used the three methods: `CreateText()`, `AppendText()` and `Exist()`.

The methods of the `File` class need to be passed a string argument indicating the directory path and file name. The directory separators take the form of a double backslash `"\\"`.

The `File` class has many other useful capabilities. Its `GetAttributes()` method retrieve a file's attributes, `Delete()` deletes a file, `Move()` and `Copy()` move or copy a file. In fact, I could have used `File.Copy()` to do all the copying which I laboriously coded in the *Streams* project. Of course, if I had done that, I would not have had the opportunity to try out the `Stream` and `StreamReader` classes. See the `FileTestBtn_Click` method in the *Streams* project for an example of using `File.Copy()`.

You may need to use `Stream` and its descendant classes when you want to process or save data from user-defined objects. So, while the `File` methods are useful to know about, they are no substitute for a full grasp of the inner life of .NET's streams!

The Directory Class

The `Directory` class can be used to create, move and enumerate through directories and subdirectories. It provides `static` methods which means that (just like the methods of the `File` class) you do not need to create an object from the class in order to use its methods. Take a look at the `dirBtn_Click()` method in the *Dir* project (on the next page).

This method retrieves the names of the drives that are active or 'mapped' to a drive identifier on your system. It calls `Directory.GetLogicalDrives()` method to initialize a string array of the drive names:

```
drives = Directory.GetLogicalDrives();
```

To display the drive names, the code iterates through the strings using a `foreach` loop:

```
foreach (string drive in drives) {
    textBox1.AppendText(drive + "\r\n");
}
```

Retrieving the name of the currently active directory is even simpler.

```
currdir = Directory.GetCurrentDirectory();
```

If you want to find the top-level directory, you can use the `GetDirectoryRoot()` method, passing to it a string that represents the path of a file or directory. My code uses the `currdir` string, which I have already initialized to the current directory:

```
dirroot = Directory.GetDirectoryRoot(currdir);
```

Dir

```
private void dirBtn_Click(object sender, System.EventArgs e) {
    string[] drives;
    string currdir;
    string dirroot;
    string[] subdirs;
    string pfdir;
    string sysdir;

    textBox1.Clear();
    // Drives
    try {
        drives = Directory.GetLogicalDrives();
        foreach (string drive in drives) {
            textBox1.AppendText(drive + "\r\n");
        }
    } catch (Exception ex) {
        textBox1.AppendText(ex.Message + "\r\n");
    }

    // Current Directory
    currdir = Directory.GetCurrentDirectory();
    textBox1.AppendText("GetCurrentDirectory() = " + currdir + "\r\n");

    // Root (top-level) directory
    dirroot = Directory.GetDirectoryRoot(currdir);
    textBox1.AppendText("GetDirectoryRoot() = " + dirroot + "\r\n");

    // SubDirectories
    subdirs = Directory.GetDirectories(dirroot);
    foreach (string sd in subdirs) {
        textBox1.AppendText(sd + "\r\n");
    }

    // Program Files Dir
    pfdir = Environment.GetFolderPath(Environment.SpecialFolder.ProgramFiles);
    textBox1.AppendText("Program Files Dir = " + pfdir + "\r\n");

    // System Dir
    sysdir = Environment.SystemDirectory;
    textBox1.AppendText("System Dir = " + sysdir + "\r\n");
}
```

try...catch

Notice that I've enclosed the code that attempts to access the drives in blocks that start with the `try` and `catch` keywords. This is a simple example of 'exception handling' to deal with potential errors. Exception handling is the subject of Chapter 9.

If you want to retrieve the names of subdirectories, use the `GetDirectories()` method to return an array of strings. Then use a `foreach` loop to iterate through them. My code iterates through all the directories immediately below the root:

```
subdirs = Directory.GetDirectories(dirroot);
foreach (string sd in subdirs) {
    textBox1.AppendText(sd + "\r\n");
}
```

Use the `Environment` class to obtain paths to special directories such as the System or Program Files directories. The `Directory` class can be used to work with the files or subdirectories in those directories. For example, this code will display the top-level subdirectories under the 'root' folder of your hard disk:

```
subdirs = Directory.GetDirectories(dirroot);
foreach (string sd in subdirs) {
    textBox1.AppendText(sd + "\r\n");
}
```

The Path Class

Having obtained a string that represents the full path to a file or directory, you may want to do certain operations such as parse out the file name or the file extension or the path (the directories and subdirectories) *minus* the file name. The `Path` class has these and other capabilities built in.

The `pathBtn_Click()` method in the *Dir* project starts by getting the path to the executable file of the `Dir.exe` program itself (the program that is created when you compile or run this project). The `ExecutablePath` property of the `Application` class supplies this:

Dir

```
string path = Application.ExecutablePath;
```

Now that you have a variable initialized with this path, you may want to find the directory name, *minus* the executable file name. To do that you can pass the `path` variable to the `GetDirectoryName()` method of the `Path` class as follows:

```
Path.GetDirectoryName(path);
```

In a similar manner, you can pass the `path` variable to other methods of the `Path` class such as:

```
GetExtension()
GetFileName()
GetFileNameWithoutExtension()
GetPathRoot()
```

This is how you would do that in C# code:

```
Path.GetExtension(path);
Path.GetFileName(path);
Path.GetFileNameWithoutExtension(path);
Path.GetPathRoot(path);
```

Each of these methods returns a modified version of the original string. The names of the methods are self-explanatory and you can view the results by running the *Dir* project and clicking the 'Path Test' button:

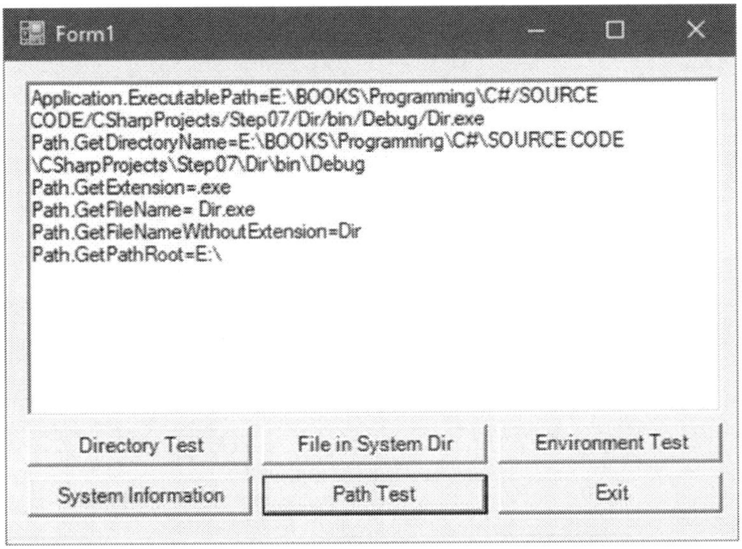

8 – Classes and Structs

In this chapter, we look at some additional features of classes as well as structures (*structs*) and enumerations (*enums*).

I've mentioned previously (see Chapter 5) that it is often considered good practice to give each class its own code file rather than to put multiple classes into a single code file. For example, if you create a class named `MyClass` you can write its code in a file named *MyClass.cs* and avoid adding any other classes to that file. That's fine for fairly small classes. But what if you write a class that contains many hundreds, or thousands, of lines of code? In that case, it might be convenient to write the code in *more than one* file.

One Class Across Multiple Code Files

While it is generally preferable to keep classes small, sometimes a complicated class may extend over many 'screenfulls' of text which make your code hard to navigate. In that case, you can divide one class across several different files. You do this by preceding the class name with the keyword `partial`.

Partial Classes

There is an example of a partial class in the *ClassesAndMore* project. You will find this code in the code file *MyClass.cs*:

ClassesAndMore [MyClass.cs]

```
partial class MyClass {
    private string _str = "";

    public MyClass() {
        _str = "A Default String";
    }

    public MyClass(string aString) {
        _str = aString;
    }
```

ClassesAndMore [MyClass.cs] (continued)

```
    public static string ToUppCase(string aString) {
        return aString.ToUpper();
    }

    public static string ToLowCase(string aString) {
        return aString.ToLower();
    }

    public static string ToLowCase(string aString, string anotherString) {
        return ToLowCase(aString)+ToLowCase(anotherString);
    }

    public string ToLowCase() {
        return ToLowCase(_str);
    }

    private string Reverse(string aString) {
        string revS = "";
        for (int i = aString.Length - 1; i >= 0; i--) {
            revS += aString[i];
        }
        return revS;
    }

    public string ToReversedLowCase() {
        return Reverse(ToLowCase(_str));
    }
}
```

This code is in the file *MyClass2.cs*:

ClassesAndMore [MyClass2.cs]

```
partial class MyClass {

    public static string Capitalize(string aString) {
     string s;
     char firstchar;
     s=ToLowCase(aString.Substring(1, aString.Length - 1))
     firstchar = char.ToUpper(aString[0]);
     return firstchar + s;
    }

}
```

The definition of `MyClass` is shared between the two code files shown here (*MyClass.cs* and *MyClass2.cs*). That is permitted only when a class is defined to be a `partial` class in both code files:

ClassesAndMore [MyClass.cs]

```
partial class MyClass {
```

ClassesAndMore [MyClass2.cs]

```
partial class MyClass {
```

In principle, a partial class could be shared across many more than two code files. However, if a class becomes so complex that its definition requires numerous code files, you might want to consider whether it would be neater to divide it up into one or more fairly small classes rather than putting all the code into one huge class.

Static Methods and Classes

A class may contain both ordinary methods (which are called by referring to an object) and `static` methods (which are called by referring to a class).

File class static methods

You may recall that we encountered some of the `File` class's `static` methods such `OpenRead()` and `OpenWrite()` in Chapter 7. A `static` method 'belongs' to a class whereas as normal or 'instance' method (see Chapter 5) belongs to a specific object.

Typically, 'normal' methods act upon an object's internal data (it's 'fields') while `static` methods act upon 'external' data which is passed to them for processing.

For example, the .NET `File.Exists()` method is `static`. You can pass a file name to `File.Exists()` as an argument and it returns a Boolean value, `true` or `false`, depending on whether or not the file can be found.

In `MyClass`, I've defined the method `ToUpCase()` as `static` and `ToLowCase()` as a normal (or 'instance') method. This is how I call the `static` method:

```
MyClass.ToUppCase("abC") // returns "ABC"
```

This is how I might call the normal (instance) method:

```
MyClass ob1;
string s;
ob1 = new MyClass("Hello World");
s = ob1.ToLowCase();
// s now equals "hello world"
```

Return Values Or Variables?

In my code, I don't assign the returned value to a variable, such as `s` as shown above. I just pass the value returned by the `ToLowCase()` method as an argument to the `AppendText()` function:

```
textBox1.AppendText(ob1.ToLowCase());
```

While it is common practice to omit 'unneeded' variables in this way, in more complicated programs, the use of additional variables can be very useful for debugging!

If you want to create a class that contains nothing but `static` methods you can make the class itself `static`. I've done this with the `MyStaticClass` class:

ClassesAndMore (MyStaticClass.cs)

```
namespace ClassesAndMore {

    static class MyStaticClass {
        public static string ToUppCase(string aString) {
            return aString.ToUpper();
        }
    }

}
```

A `static` class does not permit objects to be created from it. You can think of a `static` class as a named group of methods which provide some sort of related functionality that can be easily accessed by external code. The .NET framework includes several `static` classes such as `File` and `Directory`.

Overloaded Methods

In C# it is permissible to define multiple methods with the same name inside a single class. You can even create multiple constructors for a single class. Each constructor or each similarly-named method must have a different set of arguments. It is the argument list which resolves the ambiguity of the repeated names and allows C# to determine which method you intend to call.

The `MyClass` class, for example, defines three alternative methods called `ToLowCase()`. Two of these are `static` methods (these two methods return the lowercase version of one or more `string` arguments), but one of them is a normal method that returns the lowercase version of a `MyClass` object's `_str` variable:

ClassesAndMore [MyClass.cs]

```
public static string ToLowCase(string aString) {
    return aString.ToLower();
}

public static string ToLowCase(string aString, string anotherString) {
    return ToLowCase(aString) + ToLowCase(anotherString);
}

public string ToLowCase() {
    return ToLowCase(_str);
}
```

The `MyClass` class also has two constructors. The first takes no arguments and it sets a default value for `_str`. The second takes a string argument which is assigned to `_str`:

```
public MyClass() {
    _str = "A Default String";
}

public MyClass(string aString) {
    _str = aString;
}
```

The appropriate constructor will be called automatically, depending on whether or not a string argument is provided when a new `MyClass` object is created:

```
MyClass ob1;
MyClass ob2;
ob1 = new MyClass("Hello World");
ob2 = new MyClass();
```

I've created ob1 using the constructor that takes a string argument and assigns this to _str whereas ob2 has been created using a constructor that takes no arguments, so _str retains its default value. I can now display _str in lowercase by calling ToLowCase() on each object:

```
textBox1.AppendText(ob1.ToLowCase() + "\r\n");
textBox1.AppendText(ob2.ToLowCase() + "\r\n");
```

The Text of textBox1 shows this:

```
hello world
a default string
```

structs

As an alternative to a class, you may create a struct. Unlike a class, a struct cannot have descendants. In addition, its constructor cannot have an empty argument list. You will see an example of a struct in the file *MyStruct.cs*:

ClassesAndMore [MyStruct.cs]

```
public struct MyPointStruct {
    int _x;
    int _y;

    public MyPointStruct(int anX, int aY) {
        _x = anX;
        _y = aY;
    }

    public int X {
        get {
            return _x;
        }
        set {
            _x = value;
        }
    }
```

ClassesAndMore [MyStruct.cs] (continued)

```
public int Y {
        get {
            return _y;
        }
        set {
            _y = value;
        }
    }

    public Point AsPoint() {
        return new Point(_x, _y);
    }
}
```

The `MyPointStruct` `struct` implements a structure that contains an `x` and a `y` coordinate, similar to a .NET `Point` which its itself a `struct`.

enums

Sometimes it may be useful to create a group of constants which is called an enumeration and is defined using the keyword `enum`. An `enum` contains a coma-separated list of identifiers between curly braces like this:

ClassesAndMore [MyEnums.cs]

```
public enum CardSuits {
    Clubs,
    Spades,
    Hearts,
    Diamonds,
    Unknown
}
```

By default, each constant is assigned a numeric value from 0 upwards. However, enums are often used simply to provide descriptive names rather than to supply associated values. The identifiers may be assigned to variables of the specific `enum` type like this:

```
CardSuits selectedSuit;
selectedSuit = CardSuits.Clubs;
```

If you want to display one of the `enum`'s identifiers as a string, you can use the `ToString()` method:

```
textBox1.Text = selectedSuit.ToString();
```

You may optionally assign specific numeric values to elements of an `enum` like this:

```
public enum PictureCards {
    Jack = 11,
    Queen = 12,
    King = 13,
    NotAPictureCard = 0
}
```

Enums are used in numerous places throughout the .NET framework. For example, if you select a control in the Form designer, you can change its docking behaviour by clicking the `Dock` property. You can anchor a control (so that its edges are auto-resized when the control containing it is resized) using the `Anchor` property. These two properties are assigned values from the `DockStyle` and `AnchorStyles` enums like this:

```
textBox1.Dock = DockStyle.Top;
textBox1.Anchor = AnchorStyles.Top;
```

You can 'combine' `enum` values using the single upright bar `|` operator. This will not necessarily result in a sensible value for all enums. However, some enums expect this sort of operation. The `AnchorStyles enum`, for example, can anchor a control at the `Bottom` and `Left` of its container like this:

```
textBox1.Anchor = AnchorStyles.Bottom | AnchorStyles.Left;
```

9 – Exception Handling

There is one important problem I have not yet considered in any depth in this book. Namely: *bugs!* In this chapter, we find out how to expect the unexpected and deal with errors.

Few programs of any ambition are completely bug-free. At least, they aren't at the outset. But, with a little care, and a lot of debugging, it should be possible to squash most of the most troublesome bugs before the end-user is let loose on your application.

In some respects you could say that the programmer's greatest enemy is the user. The trouble with users is that they don't play by the rules. Your code expects them to do one thing but they go and do something else that you hadn't even thought of.

It is your responsibility, therefore, to assume that the user will, at some time or another, do the most stupid things conceivable. That means that you have to build into your code some means of recovering from potential disaster. Fortunately, C# and .NET make this fairly easy to do using exception-handling.

Exceptions

Imagine that you've created a calculator of some kind. Naturally, you expect the user to do calculations by entering numbers. But what happens if, instead of entering 1 and 0 (the numbers: one and zero), the user enters I and O (that is, the capital *letters*: I and O)? The user may be dumb for doing that, but that's no excuse for your program to crash. After all, this could an international banking system and that program crash just lost a billion dollar transaction. Blaming the user is not going to save your job!

If you plan on having a long, happy and profitable programming career, it is definitely in your interests to make your programs as crash-proof as humanly possible, no matter how stupid the users may be.

Runtime Errors and Exception Objects

In C# and .NET, runtime errors (errors that occur when the program is running rather than those that are spotted by the compiler) are handled by *exceptions*.

As with everything else in C#, an exception is an object. When an error happens, an instance of the `Exception` class (that is, an `Exception` *object*) is created. Your code can make use of this by 'catching' the exception object and using its properties and methods.

In the *Exceptions* project, I've designed a simple calculator that is ready to be handed over to my end users, all of whom are experts at crashing computer programs. Let's see if it is easy to crash this program (run this program without the debugger - `CTRL F5`).

The first user enters "IO" (letters, not numbers) into the subtotal edit box at the top of the form, then clicks the first button, labelled '*Calc*'. Right away my program runs into a problem. An error message informs me that there is an unhandled exception.

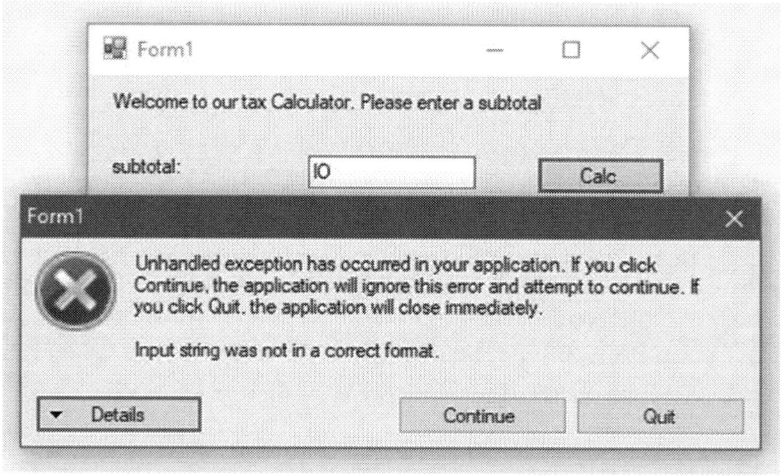

This sort of error message may be acceptable when you are *developing* an application. But is not the kind of message an end user expects to see when *running* it. Still, at least it lets me recover from the error without crashing my entire program. I can click '*Continue*' button and try again.

Now I click the second button, '*Calc2*'(with "IO" still in edit box). As before, an error occurs but now I see a different, and altogether more polite, error message. This is because the code that executes when this button is clicked 'catches' the exception object handles the exception.

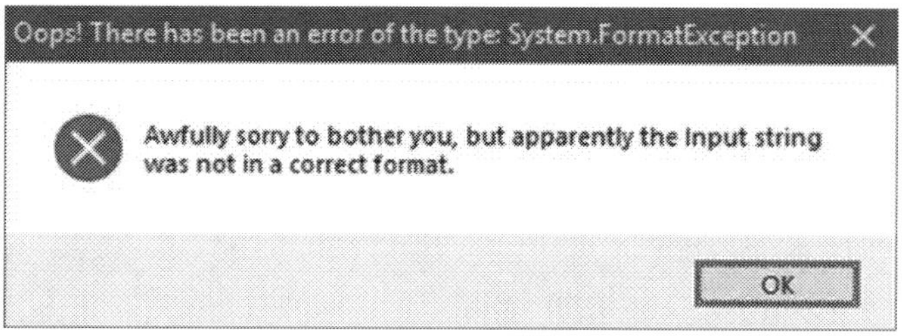

This is the code that runs when the *Calc2* button is clicked:

Exceptions

```
private void calc2Btn_Click(object sender, EventArgs e) {
    double st = 0.0;
    double tax = 0.0;
    double gt = 0.0;
    try {
        st = Convert.ToDouble(subTotBox.Text);
    } catch (Exception exc) {
        MessageBox.Show("Awfully sorry to bother you, " +
            "but apparently the " + exc.Message,
            "Oops! There has been an error of the type: " + exc.GetType(),
            MessageBoxButtons.OK, MessageBoxIcon.Error);
    }
    tax = st * 0.175;
    gt = st + tax;
    taxBox.Text = tax.ToString();
    grandTotBox.Text = gt.ToString();
}
```

The exception-handling code, which is what traps the error and deals with it, can all be found between the pairs of curly brackets after `try` and `catch`:

```
try {
    // here is code that might generate an error
} catch(Exception exc) {
    // here is code to deal with an error
}
```

In my program, the bit of code that could potentially cause a problem is the first line in the `try` block, which attempts to convert the `Text` of `subTotBox` to a `double` value:

```
try {
    st = Convert.ToDouble(subTotBox.Text);
}
```

If this conversion attempt fails (that is, if the text cannot be converted to a `double`) then the code block following the `catch` keyword is run. The `catch` block takes an argument, `exc` (the name here is not important) of the type `Exception`. When a problem occurs in the `try` block, the variable `exc` is initialized with the exception object which contains information about the error that has just occurred. This information includes a `Message` property which gives access to a string describing the error:

```
catch (Exception exc) {
     MessageBox.Show("Awfully sorry to bother you, " +
          "but apparently the " + exc.Message,
          "Oops! There has been an error of the type: " + exc.GetType(),
          MessageBoxButtons.OK, MessageBoxIcon.Error);
}
```

In the present case, `Message` provides the error string: *"Input string was not in a correct format"*. My code displays this in the message box. The exception object also has a `GetType()` method. This returns a string description of the exact error type. Here this is *"System.FormatException"*. My code displays this string in the caption of the message box.

An exception object has many other properties and methods that can provide even more detailed information on an error. Try, for example, editing the code shown above by replacing `exc.Message` with `exc.ToString()`.

Exception Types

It is also possible to catch specific *types* of exception. For an example of this, look at the code in `calc3Btn_Click()`:

Exceptions

```
private void calc3Btn_Click(object sender, EventArgs e) {
    int st = 0;
    double tax = 0.0;
    double gt = 0.0;
    try {
        st = Convert.ToInt32(subTotBox.Text);
    } catch (OverflowException exc) {
        MessageBox.Show("Try a smaller number! "
            + exc.Message,
            "Yikes! Overflow error: " + exc.GetType(),
            MessageBoxButtons.OK, MessageBoxIcon.Warning);
    } catch (Exception exc) {
        MessageBox.Show("Awfully sorry to bother you, " +
            "but apparently the " + exc.Message,
            "Oops! There seems to have been a slight " +
            "error of the type: " + exc.GetType(),
            MessageBoxButtons.OK, MessageBoxIcon.Error);
    }
    tax = st * 0.175;
    gt = st + tax;
    taxBox.Text = tax.ToString();
    grandTotBox.Text = gt.ToString();
}
```

This code expects the user to enter a 32-bit integer into `subTotBox`, the subtotal edit box. This means that if the user enters an alphanumeric character such as 'X' or a floating-point number such as 1.5, a `FormatException` will occur.

However, another type of exception is also possible. An `int32` value must fall between the range of -2,147,483,648 and 2,147,483,647. If the user enters a number larger or smaller than these values, an `OverflowException` will occur.

Try it. Enter 'X' into the subtotal box and click the *Calc3* button. You will see the same error message as previously. Now enter eleven or more digits (e.g. 999999999999) into the subtotal box and once again click *Calc3*. This time, you will see a different error message which states 'Try a smaller number!'.

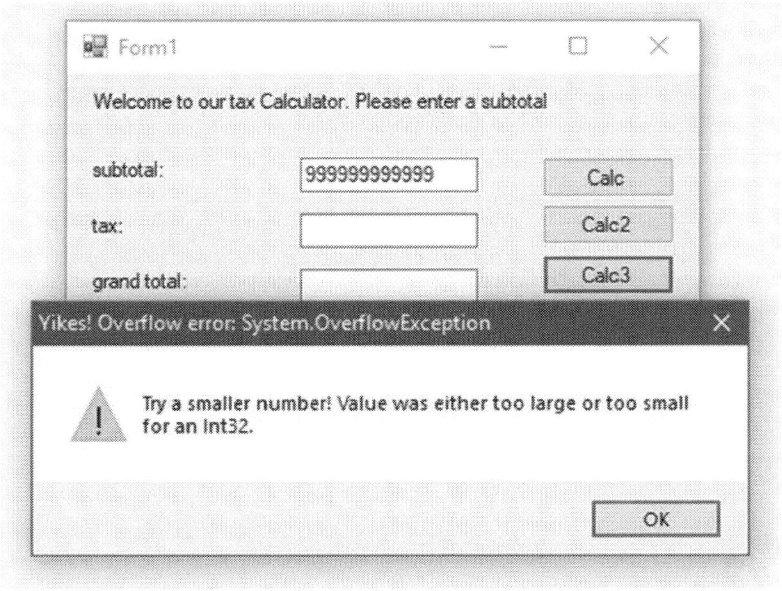

To handle a particular exception type, you need to specify that type by name in a `catch` section. In the click event-handler method for the *Calc3* button I have added a catch block to handle `OverflowException`:

```
catch (OverflowException exc) {
MessageBox.Show("Try a smaller number! "
    + exc.Message,
    "Yikes! Overflow error: " + exc.GetType(),
    MessageBoxButtons.OK, MessageBoxIcon.Warning);
}
```

I could subsequently add separate blocks specifying other type of exception such as `FormatException`. Each block will only execute if the specific type of exception object is found. If not, the code moves on to the next `catch` block. The final `catch` block should normally specify the base `Exception` class and this will execute if an exception of *any type* has occurred which has not already been handled by an earlier `catch` block.

Nested Exception Blocks

You may also nest one `try...catch` block inside another. Here's an example in which my code attempts to convert some text entered by the user into a `double`. This is in the click event-handler method for the *Calc4* button.

If the conversion fails, the exception is trapped in a `catch` block. This `catch` block assumes that the only possible cause of an error would be that the user has not entered any text:

```
try {
    st = Convert.ToDouble(subTotBox.Text);
    inputtext = subTotBox.Text;
} catch (Exception exc) {
    if (inputtext.Length == 0) {
        MessageBox.Show("You must enter some data " +
                        "into the subtotal field", "Error",
                        MessageBoxButtons.OK,
                        MessageBoxIcon.Error);
}
```

However, there is a bug in my code (yes, I hate to admit it, but that does happen sometimes!) because whenever a conversion operation fails, this line is skipped:

```
inputtext = subTotBox.Text;
```

When an exception occurs, the program immediately jumps to the `catch` block. This code here tests the length of `inputtext`. But it turns out that `inputtext` has no length because it still has the default value which I set at the top of the method, and that is `null`:

```
string inputtext = null;
```

The end result is that whenever a conversion fails in the `try` block, no matter what the reason for that failure, an unhandled exception occurs, and that is very bad news:

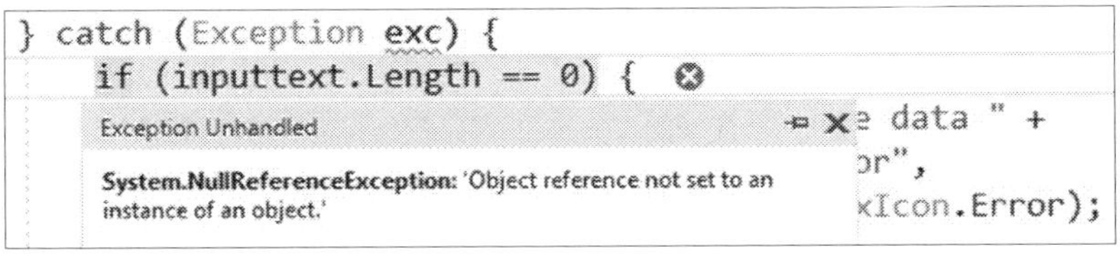

I've rewritten this code in the event-handler method for the *Calc5* button. This time, I've put the test (`inputtext.Length == 0`) inside its own `try` block:

```
 try {
    if (inputtext.Length == 0) {
         MessageBox.Show("You must enter some data into the subtotal field",
                         "Error",
                          MessageBoxButtons.OK, MessageBoxIcon.Error);
} catch (Exception exc2) {
    MessageBox.Show("Program Bug. Please contact support. Error was: " +
                          exc2.Message, "Error",
                          MessageBoxButtons.OK, MessageBoxIcon.Error);
}
```

This second exception (`exc2`) is caught by a `catch` block nested inside the `catch` block of the first exception. Now, even if two exceptions occur here, my program can recover gracefully and display an explanatory error message rather than just crashing out.

Why not just fix the bug?

The astute reader may wonder why I haven't just fixed the bug (the one that tests the length of a null value) rather than adding more exception handling. The moral of the story here is that bugs aren't always this easy to spot. At least my exception handler produces a decent bug report that can be sent back to me by the user. This will help me fix the bug more easily than just someone telling me "Your program crashed and I don't know why!"

Now, I should say here that I am not wildly keen on nested exception-handling for the simple reason that it can often be hard to understand precisely in which `catch` blocks a nested exception will be caught. Errors of all sort can be tricky to find and fix. It is my view, therefore, that error-handling should be made as simple as it possibly can be.

finally

You may optionally use a `finally` block instead of a `catch` block or place a `finally` block after one or more `catch` blocks. A `finally` block will run whether or not an exception has occurred and it may be used to reset values of any data which may be left in an unpredictable state following an exception. This `finally` block is found in the `calc5Btn_Click()` method:

Exceptions

```
try {
    // code that might cause an exception
} catch (Exception exc) {
    // code to handle exception
} finally {
    MessageBox.Show("Thank you for using our calculator", "Goodbye",
        MessageBoxButtons.OK, MessageBoxIcon.Information);
    tax = st * 0.175;
    gt = st + tax;
    taxBox.Text = tax.ToString();
    grandTotBox.Text = gt.ToString();
    statusLabel.Text = msg;
}
```

Is finally really needed?

If you handle all possible exceptions in the `try...catch` blocks of your exception handler, any code that follows it should be run as normal, even if it is not preceded by the keyword `finally`. However, a `finally` block is recommended as good practice, especially when you may want to clean up any resources that are allocated in a `try` block.

Debugging

Visual Studio has one of the best debuggers available anywhere, so be sure to make good use of it. Typically you will start a debugging session by placing breakpoints in your code to pause execution of your program at one or more points where you want to examine the values of variables. Let me now give you a quick guide to the main features of the Visual Studio Debugger. Bear in mind, however, that the Debugger has many more capabilities – far too many to describe here.

To place a breakpoint, click in the left-hand shaded margin of a code file. The breakpoint is shown as a red circle in the margin and a highlighted red line in the code.

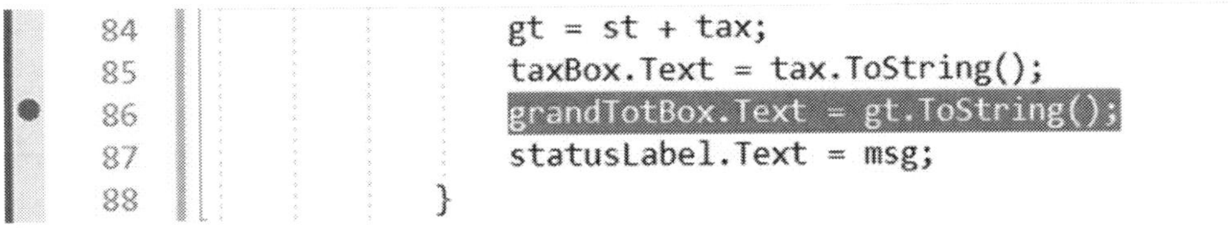

Now press **F5** to run your program in the debugger. The program will stop when a breakpoint is encountered. Use the *Locals* window to view variables that are in scope or the *Watch* window to view selected variables. You can add variables to the *Watch* window by entering them as text or by dragging them out of a code window.

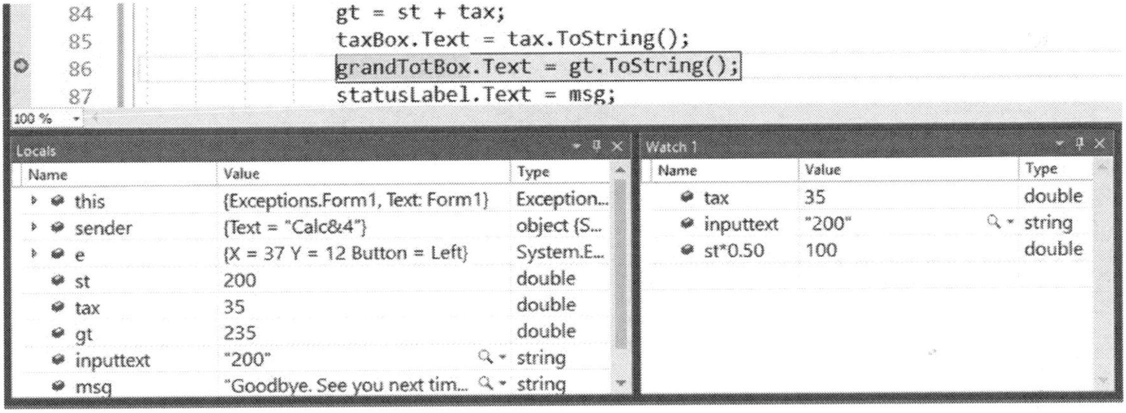

Important Debugging Keys

`F5`	*Continue Debugging* (until a breakpoint is hit)
`F10`	*Step Over* (debug to next line but don't step into any methods)
`F11`	*Step Into* (debug to next line, step into methods if necessary)
`SHIFT-F11`	*Step Out* (step to next line after the code of the current method)
`SHIFT-F5`	*Stop Debugging*

You can find debugging commands on the *Debug* menu or on the Debug Toolbar which will normally appear above the editing window during a debugging session. If the Debug toolbar is not visible, right-click the Toolbar area and select '*Debug*' from the drop-down menu.

10 – Lists and Generics

In this chapter, I plan to start work on creating an adventure game in which the player can move around a map, taking and dropping objects. Along the way we'll learn about generic lists.

I've decided I want to write a retro-style text adventure game. In order to do this, I need to manipulate lists of objects so that, for example, an item can be transferred from one list (belonging to a Room) to another list (belonging to the Player) when it is taken. To do that, I shall use some special .NET collection classes.

Generic Collections

The simplest type of list is an array which is a sequential list of items. I explained arrays in Chapter 6. In fact, the .NET framework also supplies several other collection classes such as `List` and `Dictionary`. These are called 'generic collection' classes. Let's see what they can do that arrays can't.

Lists

A `List` represents a strongly-typed collection of objects and it comes with lots of useful methods to add, remove and find objects in the collection. This is called a 'generic' list. The syntax for declaring a generic list is:

```
List<T>
```

Here `T` is the name of the type of the items in the list. In real code you might declare lists of strings or of `Thing` objects like this:

```
List<string>
List<Thing>
```

This is how I declare and construct a `List` typed to hold `Thing` objects:

```
Generics
public List<Thing> thingList = new List<Thing>();
```

I can now add a `Thing` object like this:

```
thingList.Add(new Thing("Sword", "An Elvish weapon"));
```

This is how I would remove an object at index `i`:

```
thingList.RemoveAt(i);
```

Dictionaries

The .NET Framework also has a `Dictionary` class. This is a type of list in which the items are indexed not by a sequential numerical index but by a *key* which may be a unique object of any type.

You can think of a C# `Dictionary` as the programming equivalent of a real-world dictionary in which each entry has a unique name as its '*key*' – for example, `"Dog"` – followed by a definition which is its '*value*' – for example: `"A furry mammal that woofs and gnaws on bones."`

The declaration of a `Dictionary` in C# code is a bit like the declaration of a `List` but it requires two types (the *key* and the *value*) between a pair of angle-brackets. This is how I might declare and construct a `Dictionary` with a `string` key and a `string` value, and then add a single item to it:

```
Generics
Dictionary<string, string> petDictionary = new Dictionary<string, string>();
petDictionary.Add("Dog", "A furry mammal that woofs and gnaws on bones");
```

You can try to get a value associated with a key like this:

```
string value;
petDictionary.TryGetValue("Dog", out value);
```

In this case, the `TryGetValue()` method will us the key `"Dog"` to find the associated value and it will initialize the `out value` argument to the string `"A furry mammal that woofs and gnaws on bones"`.

If the key is not found in the dictionary, `value` will be initialized with the default for the object type. Here, the `value` argument is a `string` whose default is an empty `string`. Since it would not be useful to display an empty `string` on screen, you can test the return value of the `TryGetValue()` method which will be `true` when a key is found and `false` otherwise. You will then be able to display something more useful when the key cannot be found:

```
if (petDictionary.TryGetValue("Canary", out value)) {
    textBox1.AppendText($"A Canary is {value}");
} else {
    textBox1.AppendText($"Canary is not in the dictionary");
}
```

Dictionaries can use all kinds of objects as their keys and values. This is how to declare and construct a `Dictionary` with a `string` key and `Room` value, then add a single item to it:

```
public Dictionary<string, Room> roomDictionary = new Dictionary<string, Room>();
roomDictionary.Add("Troll Room", new Room("A dank cave"));
```

Dictionaries have many other methods that they can use. In this example I use the `ContainsKey()` method to determine whether a `Dictionary` object contains a specific key and the `Remove()` method to remove an object if it exists:

```
string searchname = nameTB.Text;
if(roomDictionary.ContainsKey(searchname)) {
    roomDictionary.Remove(searchname);
}else {
    // do something else…
}
```

In the next example, my code iterates over the items in the `Dictionary` in order to access the key and the value from each item:

```
foreach (KeyValuePair<string, Room> kvp in roomDictionary) {
    s += $"{kvp.Key}: {kvp.Value.description}\r\n";
}
```

In this case, as the `Dictionary` has been typed to hold *key-value* pairs in which each *value* is a `Room` object, I am able to access each `Room` object's `description` field (a `public string` variable) from the `Value` property of the loop variable `kvp` without first having to 'cast' `Value` to a `Room`.

Overridden Methods

In an adventure game, objects of different types might need to describe themselves in different ways. That means that each class (such as `Room` and `Player`) that descends from some other class (such as the `Thing` class) will need to have a different implementation of the `Describe()` method.

Sometimes I may want to call the `Describe()` method for each object in a list of 'mixed' object types. In a complete game, for instance, a `Room` might contain some `Treasure`, `Weapon` and `Animal` objects. These objects would all be stored in a single list or dictionary.

When the player looks at the objects in a room, I might want to have a loop that iterates over objects of all these types, asking each object to describe itself. My solution to this problem is to make the `Thing.Describe()` method 'virtual':

adventure-game [Thing.cs]

```
public virtual string Describe() {
    return Name + " " + Description;
}
```

The descendant classes of `Thing` must be sure to define their own versions of this virtual method. To do this you must add the keyword `override` before the `Describe()` method name in the descendant classes like this:

```
public override string Describe()
```

virtual methods

A virtual method is one that can overridden. An overridden method is one that provides a new implementation of a method with the same name inherited from a base class. This should be clearer by the end of this chapter.

To understand why virtual methods are needed, let's consider how a normal 'non-virtual' method works. Let's suppose you have defined a class that has a method with the same name and argument list as a method of its ancestor class. Imagine, for example, that your program contains an ancestor class, `A`, and a descendant class, `B`.

A class (such as `B`) that descends from another class (such as `A`) is compatible with its ancestor. The `A` class is the ancestor of the `B` class so you could say that class `B` is a *type of* class `A`. I've written these classes in the *MethodTest* project:

MethodTest [TestClasses.cs]

```
class A {
    public string Method1() {
        return "class A: Method1\r\n";
    }

    public virtual string Method2() {
        return "class A: (virtual) Method2\r\n";
    }

    public string Method3() {
        return "class A: Method3\r\n";
    }
}

// class A is the ancestor of class B
class B : A {
    // note 'new' keyword
    public new string Method1(){
        return "class B: (new) Method1\r\n";
    }

    public override string Method2() {
        return "class B: (override) Method2\r\n";
    }

    public string Method3() {
        return "class B: Method3\r\n";
    }
}
```

In this simple example, `A.Method1()` returns the string, `"class A: Method1\r\n"` whereas `B.method1()` returns `"class B: (new) Method1\r\n"`. Instances of these classes are created as follows:

MethodTest [Form1.cs]

```
A mya1 = new A();
B myb1 = new B();
```

Were my code now to call `myb1.Method1()`, it would, of course, return the string `"class B: (new) Method1\r\n"`. But now consider what would happen if you were iterating over a collection of mixed objects, some of which might be `A` objects, others `B` objects and others (if I write some more classes) `C`, `D` and `E` objects. I'll assume that `A` is the base class – the ultimate ancestor of all other classes – and that `B` (and `C`, `D`, `E` etc.) are descendants of `A`.

Since `A` is the base class, all the objects in such as collection are either `A` objects or *descendants* of `A` objects. You could add these objects, to a generic `List`, called `oblist`, that is typed to be compatible with the `A` class:

```
List<A> oblist = new List<A>();
oblist.Add(mya1);
oblist.Add(myb1);
```

Now you write a `foreach` loop that iterates through all the objects in the list, `oblist`. This loop has to know which base type of object it is dealing with (here that's class `A`). Since all descendant objects are compatible with class `A`, it is possible to call `Method1()` for each object encountered, like this:

```
foreach(A aOb in oblist) {
    textBox1.AppendText(aOb.Method1());
}
```

Now consider what will happen if the `foreach` loop processes the `A` object `mya1` and the `B` object `myb1`. The `foreach` loop has been told that it is dealing with instances of the `A` class. When `myb1` is processed within the loop, will `b.Method1()` or `a.Method1()` be called?

Let's try it out. This is what is displayed:

```
class A: Method1
class A: Method1
```

Even though the second object is an instance of the `B` class, it is `Method1()` as defined by class `A` that is called. So all the objects processed within the loop will return the string `"class A: Method1\r\n"`, even though some of those objects may actually be *descendants* of class `A` with their own unique `Method1()` implementations.

How can we get around this problem? The answer is to make `Method1()` in the base class (`A`) a '*virtual*' method and to make `Method1()` in all the descendant objects (`B` etc.) '*overridden*' methods.

virtual and override

To do this, you need to insert the keywords `virtual` and `override` before the method type and name, like this:

```
public virtual string Method2()  {      // class A
public override string Method2() {      // class B
```

If you call the virtual `Method2()` inside the `foreach` loop, C# works out the *exact type* of the object being processed before calling the specified method. So when the `B` object, `myb1`, goes through the loop, the overridden `Method2()`(defined within the `B` class) is executed. And this is what is displayed:

```
class A: (virtual) Method2
class B: (override) Method2
```

If virtual and overridden methods are new to you, you may find this easier to understand by running (or debugging) the *MethodTest* project. You may first want to refer back to the code of my two classes, `A` and `B` (in the *TestClasses.cs* file) which appears earlier in this chapter. Notice, by the way, that I have used the `new` keyword in the definition of `Method1()` in the `B` class:

```
public new string Method1() {
    return "class B: (new) Method1\r\n";
}
```

This is recommended for clarity when an ancestor class defines a non-virtual method with the same name and argument list. When preceded by the keyword `new` a method is specifically declared to be a *replacement* for a method with the same name in its ancestor class.

In fact, if you omit the `new` keyword in a non-virtual method (as in `Method3()`), the method will operate in the same way as if the `new` keyword had been used. However, in that case, Visual Studio will show a warning.

Now look at the code of `testBtn_Click()` in the main form, *Form1.cs*, of the *MethodTest* project. The listing is shown on the next page.

MethodTest [Form1.cs]

```
private void testBtn_Click(object sender, EventArgs e) {
    A mya1 = new A();
    B myb1 = new B();

    List<A> oblist = new List<A>();
    oblist.Add(mya1);
    oblist.Add(myb1);

    textBox1.AppendText("*Calling each object specifically*\r\n");
    textBox1.AppendText(mya1.Method1());
    textBox1.AppendText(mya1.Method2());
    textBox1.AppendText(mya1.Method3());
    textBox1.AppendText(myb1.Method1());
    textBox1.AppendText(myb1.Method2());
    textBox1.AppendText(myb1.Method3());
    textBox1.AppendText("*Calling each object as an instance of class A*\r\n");
    foreach (A aOb in oblist) {
        textBox1.AppendText("Object's class is: " + aOb.ToString() + "\r\n");
        textBox1.AppendText(aOb.Method1());
        textBox1.AppendText(aOb.Method2());
        textBox1.AppendText(aOb.Method3());
    }
}
```

This displays:

```
*Calling each object specifically*
class A: Method1
class A: (virtual) Method2
class A: Method3
class B: (new) Method1
class B: (override) Method2
class B: Method3
*Calling each object as an instance of class A*
Object's class is: MethodTest.A
class A: Method1
class A: (virtual) Method2
class A: Method3
Object's class is: MethodTest.B
class A: Method1
class B: (override) Method2
class A: Method3
```

Sample Program: An Adventure Game

To end this course, I've written a small adventure game. This game lets the player move from place (`Room`) to place, taking and dropping objects:

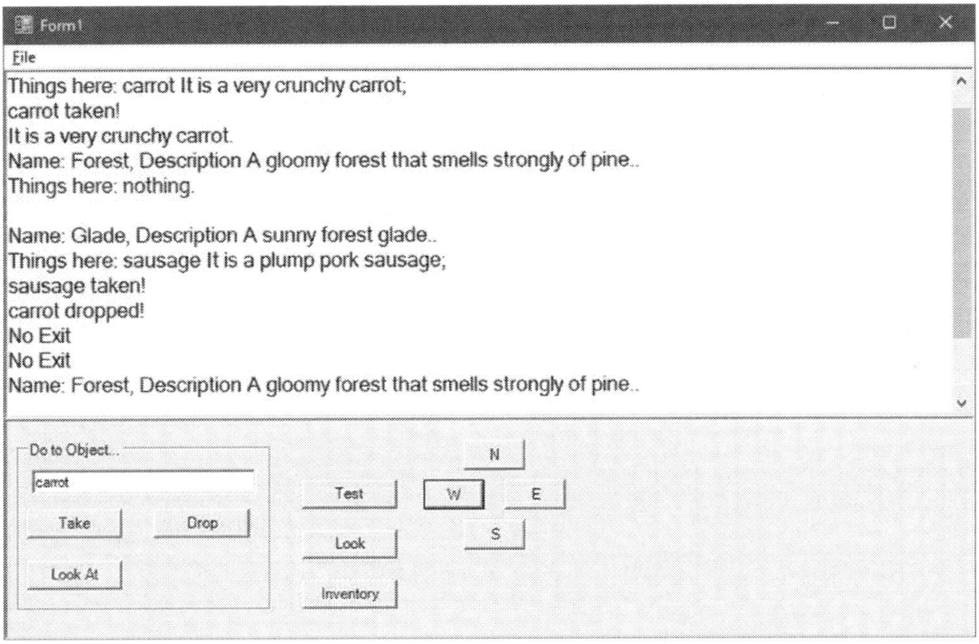

The world of the game takes the form of a map of `Room` objects.

adventure-game [Adventure.cs]

```
private RoomList _map = new RoomList();
```

The `RoomList` class here is a generic `List` typed to contain `Room` objects:

adventure-game [RoomList.cs]

```
public class RoomList : List<Room>
```

Each `Room` may itself contain a list of `Thing` objects implemented as a `ThingList`. The `ThingList` class is a generic `List` of `Thing` objects:

adventure-game [ThingList.cs]

```
public class ThingList : List<Thing>
```

I've created a special class called `ThingHolder` which has a `ThingList` as a field. Any objects that need to 'contain' a list of `Thing` objects (such as `Room`) descend from the `ThingHolder` class:

adventure-game [ThingHolder.cs]

```
public class Room : ThingHolder
```

The player can wander around the game from room to room taking and dropping objects. I am not going to explain this game in detail. It contains code that uses many of the techniques I discussed earlier in this book. You may find it useful to use this project for revision. Look through the code and, if you find anything you can't understand, refer back to the section in the book that explains those classes, methods or techniques.

The adventure-game project illustrates many of the subjects covered by this book, include class hierarchies, virtual and overridden methods (see `Describe()`), enums (see `Dir`), generic `Lists`, properties, `switch...case` tests, `foreach` loops, serialization (to save and load games) and more.

BinaryFormatter

Before leaving this game, I'd like to say a few words about how the 'game state' (the position of the player and treasure objects, for example) is saved and loaded from disk. As in previous projects, I 'serialize' objects so that they can be stored in streams. In this case I have decided to use the `BinaryFormatter` class.

This class serializes and de-serializes an object, or an entire graph or 'tree' of connected objects, in binary format. That means that I can give it a 'top level' object – one that contains many other objects, each of which may themselves contain objects – without having to bother coding all the details of saving and restoring them to and from disk.

Note too that I have had to mark all the classes I want to save with the `[Serializable]` attribute. An attribute is a special directive placed between square brackets. `BinaryFormatter` requires this attribute to be placed before the definition of any class to be serialized:

```
[Serializable]
    public class Adventure
[Serializable]
    public class Thing
[Serializable]
    public class RoomList : List<Room>
    // … and so on
```

Further Adventures In Coding

This is currently a very simple game and you can try to improve it. In fact, I'd encourage you to use my source code as a starting point and see how many new features you can add to make this into a bigger and more interesting game. See my `TODO` comments (in Visual Studio, select the *View* menu then *Other Windows* then *Task List*) for a few ideas.

To get started, I'd suggest that you take a look at the `ThingHolder` class and see if you can make it more 'self-contained' by giving it extra methods to delete objects from a list as well as add them to it. The `TransferOb()` method in the `Adventure` class could call the `ThingHolder` methods instead of using the `Add()` and `Remove()` methods of `ThingList` (which it just inherits from `List`).

You could also add new classes that descend from the `ThingHolder` class. These could be used to create 'container' objects such as treasure chests which allow the player to put other objects into them.

You may also extend the game by creating new rooms to make a bigger map. Then add more treasures and additional commands ("put treasure into container", "pull lever", "push door" and so on). And, of course, you will need to add some puzzles – limited only by your imagination.

Programming, whether it's an adventure game or something more 'serious', is a constant challenge to both your skill and your imagination. The only way to get better at it is by *doing* it, pushing the limits of your skill, sometimes succeeding, sometimes failing – and all the time learning.

Programming is an endlessly fascinating activity. I hope this little book has helped you make some progress towards mastering programming in C#. Where you take that knowledge next is entirely up to you. I wish you all the best in your programming future.

What Next?

If you'd like to extend your knowledge of C# programming even further, you might be interested in the range of online video-based programing courses from Huw Collingbourne, author of *The Little Book Of C#*. The course **Learn To Program C# in Ten Easy Steps** is the perfect complement to this book and it covers a similar range of topics in over seven hours of video and 117 lessons.

Huw also teaches courses on creating a media player (music and video) with C#, how to program a C# screen-capture utility that lets you grab picture of your whole screen, specific windows or selected rectangle. And if you are interested in retro-gaming, there is even a course on writing a C# text adventure in the style of classic games such as Zork or Colossal Cave. Huw is the author of the cult adventure game The Golden

Wombat Of Destiny and this course gives you the real inside information on writing classic-style text adventures.

In fact, you can buy the whole bundle of Huw's C# courses at a huge discount, available only to purchasers of this book.

Get the Special Deal Now on the Bitwise Courses C# bundle here:

http://www.bitwisebooks.com/special-c-sharp

Appendix

Using the Source Code

The source code of all the projects described in this book can be downloaded from the Bitwise Books web site:

http://www.bitwisebooks.com

The code is provided in a Zip archive and you will need to unzip the archive in order to extract the code into directories on your disk. The code is supplied as single Visual Studio solution which, on Windows, can be loaded directly into Microsoft Visual Studio. If you haven't got a copy of Visual Studio, you can download a free copy here:

https://visualstudio.microsoft.com/vs/community/

Online Information

For detailed documentation on the huge range of .NET classes and methods, refer to Microsoft's online documentation:

https://docs.microsoft.com/en-us/dotnet/

For more documentation on the C# language see here:

https://docs.microsoft.com/en-us/dotnet/csharp/

C# Editors and IDEs

The default – and best – IDE for programming C# is Microsoft Visual Studio on Windows. Throughout this book, I assume that you will use Visual Studio when programming C#. There are, however, several other code editors and IDEs that can be used to create and build C# projects. Some of these run on other operating systems.

Please note that the author and publisher of *The Little Book Of C#* can provide no technical help on using these tools. If you have a query or problem, you should contact the tool's developers or the join their forums to ask questions.

Visual Studio Community Edition

Visual Studio Community is a free and full-featured IDE for building apps for Web, Windows Store, Windows Desktop, and even Android and iOS using programming languages including C#, C, C++, HTML/JavaScript, and Visual Basic. At the time of writing, it is free for students, open source development, individual developers (creating *free* or *paid-for* applications) and small teams. These terms may change so if you plan to use Visual Studio for commercial development, you should refer to the Terms & Conditions on the Microsoft site:

https://www.visualstudio.com/license-terms/.

Download VS Community edition here:

https://visualstudio.microsoft.com/vs/community/

Visual Studio Code

Microsoft also has a cross-platform IDE called **Visual Studio Code**. This supports editing and debugging (but not visual design) on Windows, Linux and the Mac. It supports numerous languages including C, C++, Java, Objective-C, PHP, Python, Ruby, JavaScript and C#. More information and downloads here:

https://code.visualstudio.com/

MonoDevelop and Xamarin Studio

MonoDevelop is a cross-platform IDE that supports C# and several other languages. It runs on Mac, Linux and Windows. It includes code editing, a visual designer and debugging. The MonoDevelop project has now been merged into Xamarin Studio, which was formerly a commercial tool. MonoDevelop/Xamarin Studio is freely available on Windows, Linux and macOS. It also supports iOS and Android development. You can download MonoDevelop here:

http://www.monodevelop.com/

Visual Studio Tools for Xamarin

A set of tools and code to help you create native Android, iOS, and Windows apps using a shared .NET code base:

https://visualstudio.microsoft.com/xamarin/

Visual Studio For Mac

Microsoft is developing a product, based on Xamarin, called Visual Studio for Mac. This includes code editing, refactoring and debugging. In spite of its name, however, it is not very similar to Visual Studio on Windows:

https://www.visualstudio.com/vs/visual-studio-mac/

OmniSharp

OmniSharp is a set of open source projects that provide .NET development capabilities within a variety of editors and IDEs, including Atom, Emacs, Vim, Adobe Brackets and Sublime Text. For the latest information on OmniSharp, see the web site here:

http://www.omnisharp.net/

Frameworks and Tools

Mono

Mono is an open source, cross-platform implementation of Microsoft's .NET framework that powers cross-platform programs on Windows, Linux and OS X. You can download Mono and read more about it on the Mono Project web site:

http://www.mono-project.com/

Unity Games Development

Visual Studio for C# development with the Unity Games Engine. You will need to install Unity and the Visual Studio Unity development tools. See here:

https://visualstudio.microsoft.com/vs/unity-tools/

C# Keywords

Keywords are reserved identifiers that have special meanings to the C# compiler. They cannot be used as identifiers (for variables, constants, function names and so on) in your program unless they include `@` as a prefix. For example, `@if` is a valid identifier, but `if` is not because `if` is a keyword. Here are C#'s reserved keywords:

```
abstract, as, base, bool, break, byte, case, catch, char, checked, class, const,
continue, decimal, default, delegate, do, double, else, enum, event, explicit,
extern, false, finally, fixed, float, for, foreach, goto, if, implicit, in, int,
interface, internal, is, lock, long, namespace, new, null, object, operator,
out, override, params, private, protected, public, readonly, ref, return, sbyte,
sealed, short, sizeof, stackalloc, static, string, struct, switch, this, throw,
true, try, typeof, uint, ulong, unchecked, unsafe, ushort, using, using static,
virtual, void, volatile, while
```

For more on C# keywords, refer to Microsoft's documentation:

https://docs.microsoft.com/en-us/dotnet/csharp/language-reference/keywords/

Little Books Of ...

The Little Book Of C# is one of a series of '*Little Books Of* ...' for programmers. In each *Little Book* we aim to give you *just the stuff you really need* to get straight to the heart of the matter without all the fluff and padding.

We know that there is plenty of information online about standard code libraries, so we don't fill the pages of these books by duplicating that information. Instead, we aim to explain the really important details that you need to gain a solid understanding of each subject and start hands-on programming as quickly as possible.

Some other '*Little Books Of* ...' are:

The Little Book of Pointers

An in-depth guide to pointers in C:

- Indirection
- Pointer arithmetic
- Data Alignment
- Linked Lists (single/double)
- Stacks & Queues
- Function Pointers
- Common Pointer Problems

The Little Book of C

A beginners guide to the C language:

- Fundamentals of C
- Variable & Types
- Operators & Tests
- Functions & Arguments
- Arrays & Strings
- User-Defined Types

The Little Book of Recursion
Understanding recursion techniques in C:

- Recursive Functions
- The Call Stack
- Stack Frames
- Stack Corruption
- Recursion & Scope
- Tree Structures
- Disk Directory Recursion

You can also download a number of useful free resources from the Bitwise Books web site:

http://www.bitwisebooks.com

Manufactured by Amazon.ca
Bolton, ON

27742634R00085